Workbook for

Essentials of MMPI-2 and MMPI-A Interpretation

SECOND EDITION

James N. Butcher

University of Minnesota Press

Minneapolis • London

Published by the University of Minnesota Press
111 Third Avenue South, Suite 290
Minneapolis, MN 55401-2520
http://www.upress.umn.edu

ISBN 0-8166-3782-2

Printed in the United States of America on acid-free paper

The University of Minnesota is an equal-opportunity educator and employer.

11 10 09 08 07 06 05 04 03 02 01 00   10 9 8 7 6 5 4 3 2 1

Contents

List of Figures

Introduction

This workbook was developed with the second edition of the textbook *Essentials of MMPI-2 and MMPI-A Interpretation* to give beginning MMPI instrument interpreters additional practice in interpretation. Learning to interpret objective tests like the MMPI-2 and MMPI-A is at the same time an easy and a difficult task. It is relatively easy to gain a good basic working knowledge for interpreting the instruments because, compared with other approaches to assessing personality such as interviewing and projective techniques, the interpretive rules and strategies are spelled out and widely agreed upon. It is more difficult to acquire an in-depth knowledge of the MMPI-2 and MMPI-A if one's goals include becoming a master clinician and a clinical researcher of the instruments because of the extensive published research on the tests, which continues to grow. To be fully trained in the use of the instruments requires study beyond the introduction of *Essentials of MMPI-2 and MMPI-A Interpretation* and this workbook.

To meet the goal of providing practical introductory expertise in interpreting the MMPI-2 and MMPI-A, several strategies are followed in this workbook, ranging from reviewing or teaching basic concepts to constructing personality descriptions from the MMPI-2 and MMPI-A test results. As you will see, gaining a working knowledge of the interpretive process can be relatively uncomplicated for the beginner if it is broken up into discrete tasks. Before beginning interpretation of the MMPI-2 and MMPI-A scales, we present a test of general knowledge about the MMPI-2 and MMPI-A, followed by specific questions about the scales. Then we examine the various interpretive tasks in a sequence an interpreter might follow in organizing information derived from the different types of MMPI-2 and MMPI-A scales amply illustrated by clinical examples.

- Section 1 is a review of basic knowledge of the MMPI-2 and MMPI-A. A glossary of terms is included at the end of the workbook.
- Profile plotting and coding of the profile are addressed in Section 2. The beginning interpreter is provided raw scores for traditional validity scales L, F, and K and for the ten clinical scales for an MMPI-2 case and an MMPI-A case. The profiles should be plotted on the profile sheets; once this is done, the profile code should be constructed. Note that the primary value of coding in the interpretive process is to focus the interpreters' attention on the important elements of profile interpretation—scale elevation, profile definition, and profile configuration (shape).
- Section 3 includes exercises to explore whether a profile is valid and interpretable. The beginning interpreter is asked to examine the validity scale profile and determine whether the protocol is valid and interpretable.
- Practice in interpreting the clinical scales is given in Section 4. Several clinical scale profiles provide interpretive hypotheses about the clients. There is a brief case description for each client, giving a context for understanding the relevance of the behavioral descriptions suggested by the profiles.
- Section 5 provides the beginning interpreter with further practice in profile interpretation by incorporating relevant content themes into the clinical picture through the content scales profiles. Content-based hypotheses are considered "messages" between the client and the clinician, highlighting problems the client is acknowledging through responses to the content scales.

- Practice in interpreting the supplementary scales is offered in Section 6. Several supplementary scale profiles are furnished, and the beginning interpreter is asked to summarize the test descriptions pertinent to the cases. Brief case descriptions give the beginning interpreter a perspective on the client's problem situation.

- Interpretive exercises to integrate MMPI-2 or MMPI-A interpretation are provided in Section 7. The beginning interpreter is asked to study the full MMPI-2 or MMPI-A protocol, including the validity, clinical, content, and supplementary profiles and to develop a report summarizing the client's problems and symptoms. A brief case history for each client gives the beginning interpreter a perspective on the client's problems.

- Answers to the questions in Section 1 and sample interpretations for the interpretive sections are included in the key at the end of the workbook. Beginning interpreters can use the keys to the interpretive sections as a recommended interpretive strategy once the exercises are completed. Instructors may wish to use the key as a means of evaluating the beginning interpreter's performance in the course.

- This workbook provides practice in organizing inferences and behavioral descriptions into a diagnostic summary. If you would like to pursue the topic of writing MMPI-2 based clinical reports, see Butcher (1999); to write forensic reports, see Pope, Butcher, and Seelen (2000).

Section 1

Basic MMPI-2 and MMPI-A Constructs and Scale Information

The following terms are frequently used in MMPI-2 and MMPI-A interpretation.

Actuarial prediction

Addiction proneness

Average profile elevation

Base rate

Checkmark validity pattern

Code type

Content scale

Criterion group

Critical items

Cut-off score

Empirical correlates

Empirical scale construction

External validity

Face validity

Floating profile

Linear T score

Megargee Classification System

Neurotic triad

Percentile rank

Profile code

Profile configuration

Profile definition

Profile elevation

Submerged profile

Supplementary scale

Uniform T score

The MMPI-2 Scales

Validity Scales (See Chapter 3)

Cannot Say score (?)	The total number of unanswered items. This score can serve as an index of cooperativeness.
Variable Response Inconsistency (VRIN)	Measures the tendency to endorse items in an inconsistent or random manner.
True Response Inconsistency (TRIN)	Measures the tendency to endorse items in an inconsistent true or false manner; also detects yea-saying (responding "true") and nay-saying (responding "false").
Infrequency (F)	Measures the tendency to exaggerate psychological problems or endorse an extreme number of problems in the first part of the booklet; also detects random responding.
Infrequency Back (F_b)	Measures the tendency to exaggerate psychological problems or endorse an extreme number of problems toward the end of the booklet; also detects random responding.
Infrequency psychopathology (F_p)	Measures the tendency to endorse extreme items compared with a general psychiatric sample.
Lie (L)	Measures the tendency to claim excessive virtue or attempt to present an overall favorable image.
Defensiveness (K)	Measures the tendency to present oneself in an unrealistically positive way.
Superlative Self-presentation (S)	Measures the tendency to present oneself in an extremely positive or superlative way.
Percent True	The percentage of items that the individual has endorsed "true." This index detects yea-saying response attitudes—for example, records with greater than 30 percent of responses "true."
Percent False	The percentage of items that the individual endorsed "false." This index detects nay-saying response attitudes—for example, records with greater than 30 percent of responses "false."

Clinical Scales (See Chapter 4)

Scale 1	Hypochondriasis (Hs)	Measures excessive somatic concern and physical complaints.
Scale 2	Depression (D)	Measures low morale and symptomatic depression.
Scale 3	Hysteria (Hy)	Measures hysteroid personality features, such as having a "rose-colored glasses" view of the world and the tendency to develop physical problems under stress.
Scale 4	Psychopathic Deviate (Pd)	Measures antisocial tendencies or the tendency to act out impulsively and show poor judgment and irresponsible behavior.
Scale 5	Masculinity-Femininity (Mf)	Measures gender-role reversal or nontraditional sex-role attitudes.
Scale 6	Paranoia (Pa)	Measures suspicious, paranoid ideation, anger, and externalization of blame.
Scale 7	Psychasthenia (Pt)	Measures anxiety; obsessive, worrying behavior; and obsessive-compulsive characteristics.
Scale 8	Schizophrenia (Sc)	Measures peculiarities in thinking, feeling, and social behavior. High scores are associated with a negative self-concept and bizarre thinking.
Scale 9	Hypomania (Ma)	Measures extremely elated mood state and the tendency to yield to impulses.
Scale 0	Social Introversion (Si)	In the elevated range, this scale measures social anxiety, withdrawal, and overcontrol. In low ranges, it assesses outgoing or extroverted behavior.

Note: It is general practice to refer to a clinical scale by its number rather than the name it was given by the test authors.

Scale 1	Hypochondriasis
Scale 2	Depression
Scale 3	Hysteria
Scale 4	Psychopathic deviate
Scale 5	Masculinity-Femininity
Scale 6	Paranoia
Scale 7	Psychasthenia
Scale 8	Schizophrenia
Scale 9	Hypomania
Scale 0	Social introversion

Content Scales (See Chapter 6)

Anxiety (ANX) — Measures excessive somatic concerns and physical complaints.

Fears (FRS) — Measures specific fears or phobias.

Obsessiveness (OBS) — Measures obsessive or compulsive behavior.

Depression (DEP) — Measures subjective depression or low mood.

Health Concerns (HEA) — Measures the presentation of physical symptoms.

Bizarre Mentation (BIZ) — Measures peculiar thinking and feeling, and suspicious, paranoid ideation.

Anger (ANG) — Measures temper problems and loss of control when angry.

Cynicism (CYN) — Measures cynical attitudes and beliefs.

Antisocial Practices (ASP) — Measures antisocial behavior and practices, and problems with the law.

Type A (TPA) — Addresses the personality characteristics associated with Type A personality, such as driven behavior, rigidity, unrealistic holding to schedule, and interpersonal hostility.

Low Self-Esteem (LSE) — Measures negative self-attitudes or feelings of low self-worth.

Social Discomfort (SOD) — Measures social anxiety, withdrawal, and social behavioral problems.

Family Problems (FAM) — Addresses family relationship problems.

Work Interference (WRK) — Addresses attitudes and behaviors that reflect an unwillingness or inability to work.

Negative Treatment Indicators (TRT) — Assesses personality characteristics and attitudes that reflect noncompliance or negative attitudes toward changing one's behavior.

Selected Supplementary Scales

Addiction Proneness (APS)	Assesses the extent to which an individual's personality features match those of people in substance-use treatment.
Addiction Admission (AAS)	Assesses the extent to which an individual has acknowledged substance-abuse problems.
MacAndrew Alcoholism-Revised (MAC-R)	An empirical scale measuring proneness to becoming addicted to various substances.
Post-Traumatic Stress Disorder (PK)	Measures the tendency to claim a large number of Post-Traumatic Stress Disorder symptoms.
Hostility (Ho)	Assesses aggressive, hostile behavior and attitudes.
Anxiety (A)	A factor analytically derived scale assessing general maladjustment.
Repression (R)	A factor analytically derived scale assessing overcontrol.
Marital Distress Scale (MDS)	Assesses perceived marital relationship problems.

The MMPI-A Scales

Validity Scales (See Chapter 10)

Cannot Say score (?)	The total number of unanswered items. This score can serve as an index of cooperativeness.
Variable Response Inconsistency (VRIN)	Measures the tendency to endorse items in an inconsistent or random manner scale.
True Response Inconsistency (TRIN)	Measures the tendency to endorse items in an inconsistent true or false manner scale; also detects yea-saying (responding "true") and nay-saying (responding "false").
Infrequency 1 (F_1)	Measures the tendency to exaggerate psychological problems or endorse an extreme number of problems in the first part of the booklet; also detects random responding.
Infrequency 2 (F_2)	Measures the tendency to exaggerate psychological problems or endorse an extreme number of problems in the second part of the booklet; also detects random responding.
Infrequency (F)	Measures the tendency to exaggerate psychological problems or endorse an extreme number of problems; also detects random responding.
Lie (L)	Measures the tendency to claim excessive virtue or attempt to present an overall favorable image.
Defensiveness (K)	Measures the tendency to present oneself in an unrealistically positive way.

Clinical Scales (See Chapter 11)

See the descriptions of the MMPI-2 clinical scales earlier in this section.

Content Scales (See Chapter 12)

Adolescent-Anxiety (A-anx)	Measures excessive somatic concern and physical complaints.
Adolescent-Obsessiveness (A-obs)	Measures obsessive or compulsive behavior.
Adolescent-Depression (A-dep)	Measures subjective depression or low mood.
Adolescent–Health Concerns (A-hea)	Assesses the presentation of physical symptoms.
Adolescent-Alienation (A-aln)	Assesses the feeling of being distant from others and not cared for by them.
Adolescent–Bizarre Mentation (A-biz)	Measures peculiar thinking and feeling, and suspicious, paranoid ideation.
Adolescent-Anger (A-ang)	Measures temper problems and loss of control when angry.
Adolescent-Cynicism (A-cyn)	Assesses cynical attitudes and beliefs.
Adolescent–Conduct Problems (A-con)	Measures antisocial behavior and practices, and problems with the law.
Adolescent–Low Self-Esteem (A-lse)	Assesses negative self-attitudes or feelings of low self-worth.
Adolescent–Low Aspirations (A-las)	Assesses interest and participation in life activities.
Adolescent–Social Discomfort (A-sod)	Measures social anxiety, withdrawal, and social behavioral problems.
Adolescent–Family Problems (A-fam)	Assesses family relationship problems.
Adolescent–School Problems (A-sch)	Assesses attitudes and behavior relating to school performance.
Adolescent–Negative Treatment Indicators (A-trt)	Assesses personality characteristics and attitudes that reflect noncompliance with or negative attitudes toward changing one's behavior.

Supplementary Scales

Alcohol/Drug Problem Proneness (PRO)	Assesses the extent to which an adolescent's personality features match those of people in substance-use treatment.
Alcohol/Drug Problem Acknowledgment (ACK)	Assesses the extent to which an adolescent has acknowledged substance-abuse problems.
MacAndrew Addiction Scale (MAC-R)	An empirical scale measuring proneness to becoming addicted to various substances.
Anxiety (A)	A factor analytically derived scale that assesses general maladjustment.
Repression (R)	A factor analytically derived scale that assesses overcontrol.

Exercise: MMPI-2 and MMPI-A Concepts

The two parts of this exercise present questions regarding background knowledge of the MMPI-2 and MMPI-A. Part A concerns general knowledge about the tests; Part B focuses on information about particular scales. Answers are given in the key at the end of the workbook.

Part A. Fill in the blank with the most appropriate term.

1. An MMPI-2 _____ is a summary index that is made up of a combination of two or more scales in the clinical profile.

2. _____ are MMPI-2 psychometric measures that assess unitary dimensions or content themes.

3. The _____ scale was an empirical scale constructed by Hathaway and McKinley for the original MMPI to assess differences between hypochondriacal patients and normals.

4. _____ items are often valuable in providing clues to particular problems or symptoms that the client has endorsed.

5. In addition to assessing problem themes, the _____ are also valuable as predictors of external behaviors, as are the clinical scales.

6. The frequency at which a particular disorder occurs in a given population is referred to as the _____ of the disorder.

7. Behaviors or symptoms that are found to be associated with a particular scale score are referred to as _____.

8. A norming method that made comparable percentile values for a given T score possible for all MMPI-2 scale distributions: _____.

9. A construct on which the MAC-R scale of the MMPI-2 was based is _____.

10. A method of developing personality scales by selecting items that differentiate a defined group from a control group is referred to as _____.

11. The concept of _____ refers to the degree of "distance" between a high point score and the next highest scale score in a profile.

12. Profile _____ is the shape of the clinical profile or the pattern of scales defining the relationships among the clinical scales.

13. Profile _____ is a term that describes how "clear" or "unambiguous" a scale peak or code type is.

14. The rational scale construction strategy involves selecting items based on _____ validity.

15. The clinical scales of the original MMPI were based on _____ T scores.

16. A 2-7/7-2 pattern is referred to as a two-point _____.

17. Clinicians who use the MMPI-2 in clinical assessment typically describe their clients in terms of _____.

18. The _____ and _____ on the MMPI-2 are thought to be direct communications between the client and the clinician.

19. _____ is at the heart of computer-based personality assessment.

20. The formula $T = 50 + [10(X - MEAN)] / SD$

    where
    X = each raw score that could potentially be obtained by a given MMPI-2 scale
    MEAN = the mean raw score among subjects for that scale
    SD = the standard deviation among subjects for that scale

    is the statistical formula for _____.

21. A collection of cases that are judged to have the same characteristics in empirical item selection is referred to as a _____.

22. The first three clinical scales (Hs, D, and Hy) are referred to as the _____.

23. The MMPI-A is recommended for adolescents between the ages of _____ and _____.

24. A total of _____ couples from the MMPI-2 normative study provided personality ratings of each other to serve as validation information for the scales.

25. The MMPI-2 normative sample consisted of _____ persons drawn at random from sites across the United States.

26. _____ T scores ensure that the MMPI-2 percentile values are comparable across the scales.

27. Personality descriptions such as impulsive, low-frustration tolerance, and irresponsible behavior are _____ of the Pd scale.

28. The symbol to represent a T score of 65 in the MMPI-2 profile code is _____.

29. The symbol to represent a T score of 90 to 99 in the MMPI-2 profile code is _____.

30. A T-score elevation of 80 is _____ standard deviations above the mean of the scale.

31. The fact that MMPI-2 clinical scores are uniform means that a particular T score falls at approximately the same _____.

32. Computer-administered tests (are or are not) comparable to paper and pencil administered tests.

33. If an adult has completed a minimum of _____ items on the MMPI-2, then the original validity (L, F, and K) scales and the clinical scales can be scored.

34. If an adolescent has completed a minimum of _____ items on the MMPI-A, then the original validity (L, F, and K) scales and the clinical scales can be scored.

35. The MMPI-2 classification system for felons is called the _____.

36. The arithmetic mean of the scales Hs, D, Hy, Pd, Pa, Sc, and Ma is the _____.

37. A-las is an MMPI-A _____ scale.

38. _____ has traditionally been shown to be more effective than clinical prediction.

39. Most MMPI-2 and MMPI-A scales use _____ T scores.

40. A T score of 65 falls at about the _____ percentile for both men and women.

41. _____ are viewed as direct communications between the client and the clinician.

42. The APS scale, like the MAC-R, is a measure of _____.

43. The MMPI clinical scales were constructed originally according to an _____strategy.

44. Scales O-H and MDS are referred to as _____.

45. In addition to having _____, the MMPI-2 content scales have been found to have predictive validity.

46. A somewhat arbitrary point in an MMPI-2 or MMPI-A scale distribution at which a particular interpretation or decision is made is a _____ score.

47. A T score of 70 is _____ standard deviations above the mean.

48. A _____ profile is one that has no points at or above a T score of 50.

49. A _____ profile is one in which the L and K scores are elevated above the F scale.

50. A _____ profile is one in which all the clinical scales and Mf and Si have scores above a T score of 65.

Part B. Fill in the blank with the most appropriate scale information.

1. The _____ scale was developed as an MMPI-2 measure of the tendency for people to deny or minimize their substance use or abuse.

2. Which two MMPI-2 clinical scales assess problems of somatization? _____ and _____

3. Although the _____ content scale and the _____ clinical scale have similar names, they do not assess exactly the same personality and clinical features.

4. The most pertinent and universal descriptor for scale 7 (Psychasthenia) is _____.

5. Relationship problems are most directly assessed by the _____ scale.

6. Skeptical beliefs about other people are most directly appraised by the _____ scale.

7. The first published scale of the MMPI (1940), which addressed somatic complaints, was named the _____ scale.

8. When the _____ scale is significantly elevated, the client is likely to show suspicion, mistrust, and a tendency to externalize blame.

9. The _____ scale was developed as a means of assessing the tendency to claim excessive virtue.

10. The name of Scale 9 is _____.

11. The _____ scale was developed as a means of evaluating suspicion, mistrust, and interpersonal hyper-sensitivity.

12. The _____ scale was developed as a means of assessing factors related to sex role identification.

13. The _____ scale assesses the personality characteristics of inhibition, social withdrawal, and shyness.

14. The _____ scale was developed as a means of appraising test defensiveness.

15. The _____ scale was designed as a measure of test defensiveness on the MMPI-2 and provides a means of examining facets of defensive responding.

16. The _____ scale is an effective measure of inconsistency that addresses random responding.

17. The _____ scale on the MMPI-A measures the tendency of some adolescents to show a low level of aspiration in life.

18. Adolescents who have problems in family relationships tend to score high on the _____ content scale.

19. Adolescents who have feelings of alienation and self-doubt will likely score high on clinical scale _____.

20. APS is a supplementary scale in the MMPI-2 that addresses problems of _____.

21. The Mf scale on the standard profile assesses traditional _____.

22. Very high _____ scale (clinical) elevations are often associated with the tendency to have scrapes with the law, irresponsible attitudes, and impulsive behavior.

23. The K correction that is applied to Scale 4 is _____.

24. The K correction that is applied to Scale 1 is _____.

25. The K correction that is applied to Scale 8 is _____.

26. The MMPI-A clinical scales (are or are not) K corrected as are five scales in the MMPI-2.

27. The Dissimulation Index developed by Gough to assess exaggerated symptom checking is the raw score of _____ minus the raw score of _____.

28. An excessive number of "false" responses (greater than _____ percent) will result in an invalid record.

29. Persons who are defensive, careless, indecisive, or uncooperative may produce high numbers of _____.

30. All of the L scale items are answered in the _____ direction.

31. The _____ scale assesses superlative self-presentation and correlates highly with the _____ scale.

32. The _____ scale provides an assessment of extreme item endorsement compared to a psychiatric sample.

33. A score of 79 or less on the _____ scale (assuming low Cannot Say scores) is a clear indication of consistent and nonrandom responding.

34. Scores of 90+ on the _____ scale provide a strong indication of exaggerated (malingered) responding—much more extreme and exaggerated symptom claiming than is found in a psychiatric sample.

35. The AAS scale was developed to assess _____.

36. The S scale was designed to assess _____.

37. The F_p scale was developed to assess _____ in a psychiatric sample.

38. The tendency for some people to be very difficult to get along with and to be viewed by others as hostile is assessed by the supplementary Scale _____.

39. The _____ scale was developed by Welsh to assess the first main factor of the MMPI.

40. The _____ scale was developed by Welsh to assess the second main factor of the MMPI.

41. _____, a supplementary scale, provides a summary of the client's acknowledgment of relationship problems.

42. The _____ scale was published on the original MMPI to assess symptoms and problems related to suspicion, mistrust, and paranoid thinking.

43. The _____ clinical scale was constructed by empirical scale development procedures but was refined by the use of internal consistency statistics. It is essentially a marker of the first factor of the MMPI.

44. A basic scale on the original MMPI basic profile, the _____ scale assesses social extroversion.

45. The A-lse content scale measures _____ in adolescents.

46. The _____ content scale measures behavioral or conduct problems in adolescents.

47. The _____ scale measures an adolescent's admission of alcohol or drug problems.

48. The _____ content scale assesses an adolescent's perception of having school-related problems.

49. The MAC-R scale, developed on an adult male Veterans Affairs population, assesses _____ in adolescents as well.

50. The name of the MMPI-A content scale that assesses unusual or psychotic mentation is _____.

When you are satisfied that you have sufficient basic knowledge and background information about the MMPI-2 and MMPI-A, you are ready to turn to the various interpretive tasks.

Section 2

Exercise: Plotting and Coding Profiles

Psychologists learning MMPI-2 and MMPI-A interpretation are initially asked to learn how to plot the profile from raw scores and then code the profile, in order to become aware of the nuances of configuration, elevation, and definition in the interpretation of the clinical profile. This section provides exercises to help the beginning interpreter become accustomed to organizing the MMPI-2 and MMPI-A profile information necessary to conduct an interpretive evaluation. One MMPI-2 profile and one MMPI-A profile are presented. The initial phase of MMPI-2 or MMPI-A interpretation involves plotting the profile if the test is hand-scored.

The steps in plotting the profile are as follows:

- determine the raw scores, K corrected when appropriate;
- place the raw scores on the profile form;
- code the profile; and
- determine what MMPI-2 or MMPI-A clinical variables should be examined further for interpretation.

When you are interpreting the MMPI-2, keep in mind that there are currently different forms of the basic scales profile. The ordering of the validity scales may vary. We will present several forms of the profile in this workbook.

Case 1 (MMPI-2)

Plotting an MMPI-2 profile. Plot the following raw scores on the blank MMPI-2 profile in Figure 1. Make sure that you have included the corrected K values when necessary. The client is male.

Scale		Raw Score
Scale L	Lie	9
Scale F	Infrequency	39
Scale K	Defensiveness	25
Scale 1	Hypochondriasis	2
Scale 2	Depression	19
Scale 3	Hysteria	28
Scale 4	Psychopathic Deviate	20
Scale 5	Masculinity-Femininity	27
Scale 6	Paranoia	15
Scale 7	Psychasthenia	7
Scale 8	Schizophrenia	4
Scale 9	Hypomania	11
Scale 0	Social Introversion	21

MMPI-2™ S.R. Hathaway and J.C. McKinley

Minnesota Multiphasic Personality Inventory-2™

Profile for Basic Scales

Name ____________________

Address ____________________

Occupation ____________________ Date Tested __/__/__

Education ________ Age ________ Marital Status ____________

Referred By ____________________

MMPI-2 Code ____________________

Scorer's Initials ____________________

Fractions of K

K	.5	.4	.2
30	15	12	6
29	15	12	6
28	14	11	6
27	14	11	5
26	13	10	5
25	13	10	5
24	12	10	5
23	12	9	5
22	11	9	4
21	11	8	4
20	10	8	4
19	10	8	4
18	9	7	4
17	9	7	3
16	8	6	3
15	8	6	3
14	7	6	3
13	7	5	3
12	6	5	2
11	6	4	2
10	5	4	2
9	5	4	2
8	4	3	2
7	4	3	1
6	3	2	1
5	3	2	1
4	2	2	1
3	2	1	1
2	1	1	0
1	1	0	0
0	0	0	0

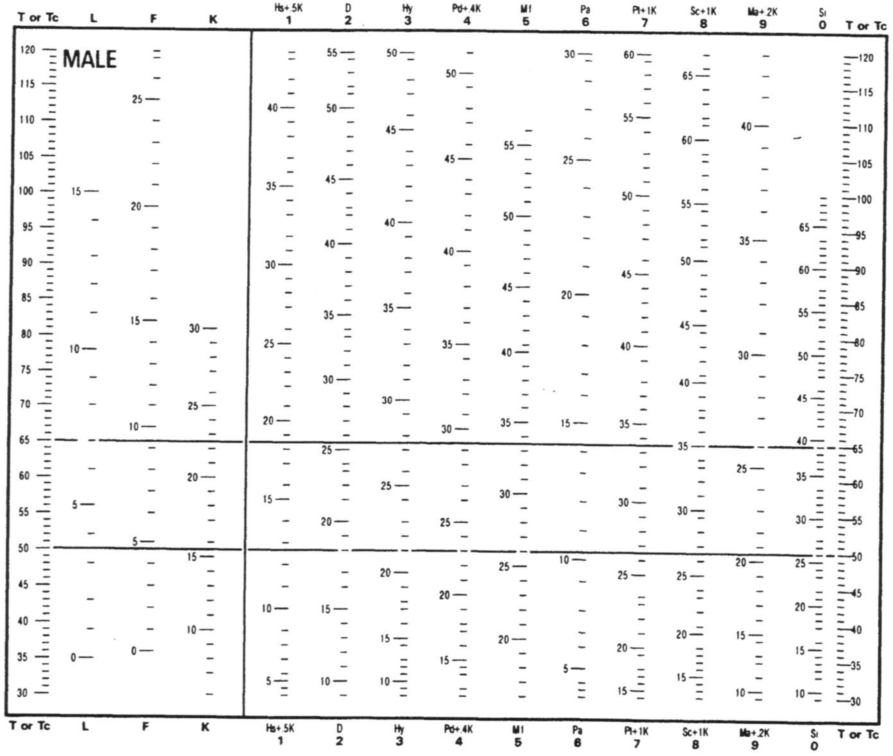

Raw Score ___

? Raw Score ___

K to be Added ___

Raw Score with K ___

NATIONAL COMPUTER SYSTEMS

24001

Figure 1. MMPI-2 basic scales profile form for Case 1.

Part A. Determining the K-corrected scores

What are the values of K to be added to the raw scores of the scales that require K correction in this case? (Refer to the box on the left of the hand-scoring profile sheet in Figure 1 to locate the percentage of K to be added to the K-corrected scales.)

Hs _____

Pd _____

Pt _____

Sc _____

Ma _____

Part B. Coding an MMPI-2 profile

Now that you have plotted the profile, the next step is to "summarize" the profile information by coding it. What is the code for this profile? (See pages 32–35 of *Essentials*.)

Part C. Correlates for the profile

Develop a list of the most appropriate correlates for this profile.

As you search the empirical interpretive literature for your report on this case, which clinical scale elevation or two- or three-point code type do you consider important to focus on for this profile?

Case 2 (MMPI-A)

Plot the following raw scores on the MMPI-A profile in Figure 2. The client is male.

Scale		Raw Score
Scale L	Lie	1
Scale F	Infrequency	10
Scale K	Defensiveness	12
Scale 1	Hypochondriasis	16
Scale 2	Depression	24
Scale 3	Hysteria	37
Scale 4	Psychopathic Deviate	34
Scale 5	Masculinity-Femininity	22
Scale 6	Paranoia	20
Scale 7	Psychasthenia	33
Scale 8	Schizophrenia	39
Scale 9	Hypomania	27
Scale 0	Social Introversion	19

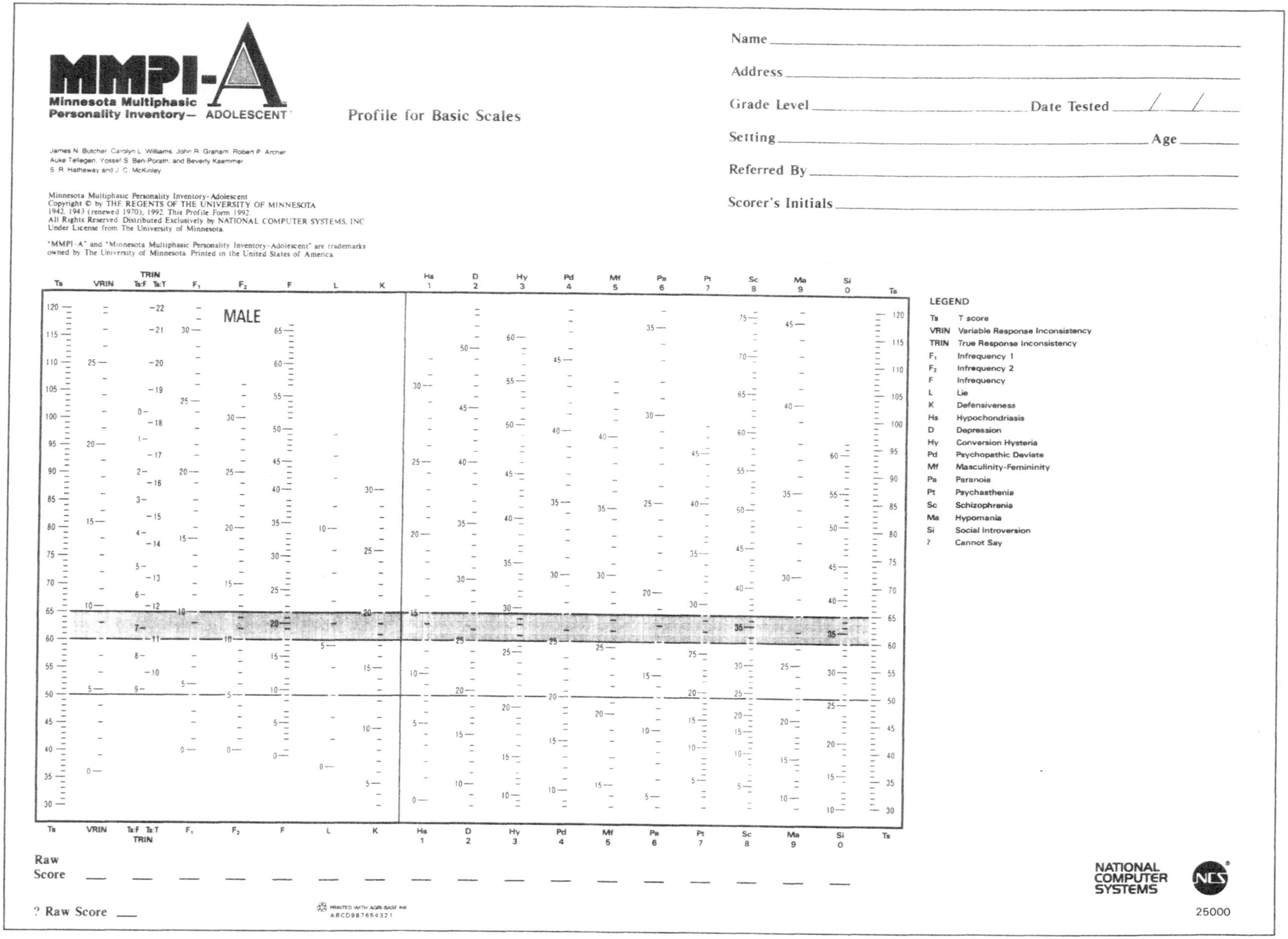

Figure 2. MMPI-A basic scales profile form for Case 2.

Part A. K correction

Is there a K correction for MMPI-A scores?   Yes _____   No _____

Part B. Profile coding

What is the code for this profile?

Part C. Clinical scale

When developing your report, which clinical scale would you consider most important to search for in the empirical interpretive literature?

Section 3

Interpreting Profile Validity

Validity Scale Factors to Address in Judging Whether a Profile Can Be Interpreted

The next step in the interpretation process is to determine whether the profile is interpretable, based on information in the validity scale pattern. Be familiar with Chapters 3 and 10 before completing this section.

The following questions will help you determine whether the profile is valid and interpretable.

1. Has the client followed the instructions in responding to the inventory? Were all or most of the items responded to? Did the individual complete a sufficient number of items to produce a usable, valid self-report? If a number of items were omitted, were there any particular content themes in the items omitted? Were some scales more affected by the item omissions than others—that is, were there differential response rates for the different scales?

2. Did the client produce any unusual patterns of responding? For example, what was the percentage of True responses and percentage of False responses? Does this profile reflect an "All True" or "All False" response pattern? If so, the profile will provide no useful information.

3. Did the client respond to the items consistently, that is, answer similar items in similar ways? Examine the scores of the inconsistency scales VRIN and TRIN. If either scale has a T score above 80, consider the possibility that the client has not attended carefully to the test items.

4. Evaluate the client's cooperativeness with the testing by determining whether he or she presented an unrealistically positive self-report. If the L score was equal to or greater than T = 65, the individual is considered to have been claiming more "virtue" than most people do and minimizing or denying problems. Raise questions about why the individual might be presenting an overly positive self-view.

5. Determine if the client responded defensively to the items by looking at the scores on the K and S scales. If these measures are elevated above a T score of 65, then consider the possibility that the client has presented himself or herself in an overly positive manner.

6. If the client has scored in the significant range (above a T score of 65) on any of the S subscales, evaluate the particular themes or manner in which they are being defensive. Which S subscales are elevated above a T score of 65? Is most of the S scale elevation accounted for by a single subscale elevation, such as S4 (Denial of Irritability and Anger)? If so, then this problem area might be considered to have more significance for the client.

7. Does the client show signs of exaggerated responding on validity scales F, F_b, or F_p? T scores in the 60–80 range may mean that the individual is simply endorsing a number of mental health problems. Scores that range higher, however, particularly those over a T score of 90, are considered to reflect symptom exaggeration. Scales in the 100+ range are thought to reflect a malingering of mental health symptoms. The individual may be claiming to have mental health symptoms to gain services or benefits.

8. Does the client's test response pattern reflect such a wide array of symptoms that it is an unlikely profile, even in a mental health facility? What is the elevation on F_p? Extreme elevations (over a T score of 80) on this scale may mean the individual has endorsed an unrealistically broad range of mental health symptoms, unlikely to be found in samples of psychiatric patients.

In cases 3–6 in this section, indicate:

(a) the score "level" of each measure

(b) the most appropriate description for each score from the following (choose one):
- clearly valid
- probably valid
- somewhat elevated, interpretable
- moderately elevated, probably interpretable
- highly elevated—possibly invalid
- extremely elevated—probably invalid
- clearly invalid

(c) whether you think the profile is valid and interpretable or what pattern of invalidity is present.

Case 3 (MMPI-2)

Case description: Mr. D. was evaluated in the context of a child-custody evaluation. He is a 40-year-old fast-food restaurant manager, currently divorced, and father of two preteen girls. He was taking the MMPI-2 at the insistence of the family court referee because of allegations that he may have sexually abused his older daughter (age 9).

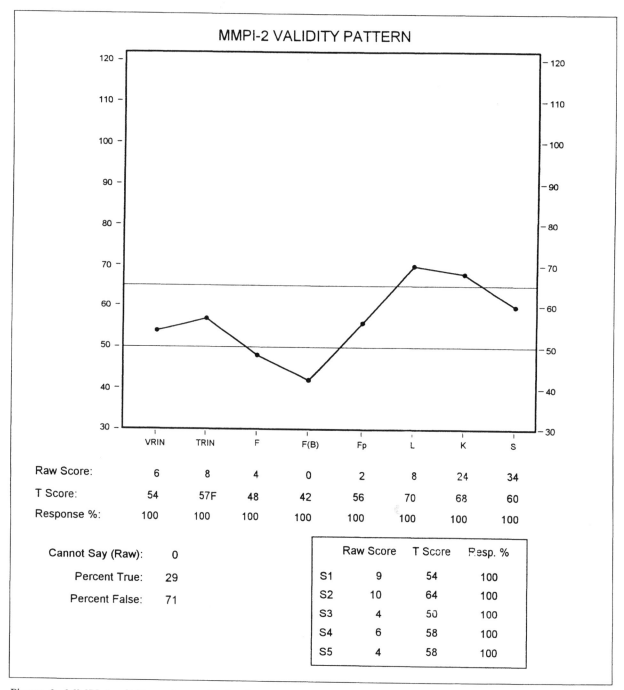

Figure 3. MMPI-2 validity scales profile for Case 3 (Mr. D.).

		(a)	(b)
Scale		**Level**	**Decision**
?	Cannot Say		
VRIN	Variable Response Inconsistency		
TRIN	True Response Inconsistency		
F	Infrequency		
F_b	Infrequency Back		
F_p	Infrequency Psychopathology		
L	Lie		
K	Defensiveness		
S	Superlative Self-Presentation		

(c) Given this validity profile configuration, are the other MMPI-2 scales interpretable? If not, why not?

_____

_____

_____

_____

_____

_____

_____

_____

_____

Case 4 (MMPI-2)

Case description: Elaine C., a 27-year-old woman, was evaluated as part of a personal injury lawsuit she filed against her employer. She claimed to have been discriminated against and subjected to hardship by her supervisor following her rejection of sexual advances he allegedly made toward her. She alleges that she has experienced retaliation and a hostile work environment to the point that she has developed symptoms of PTSD.

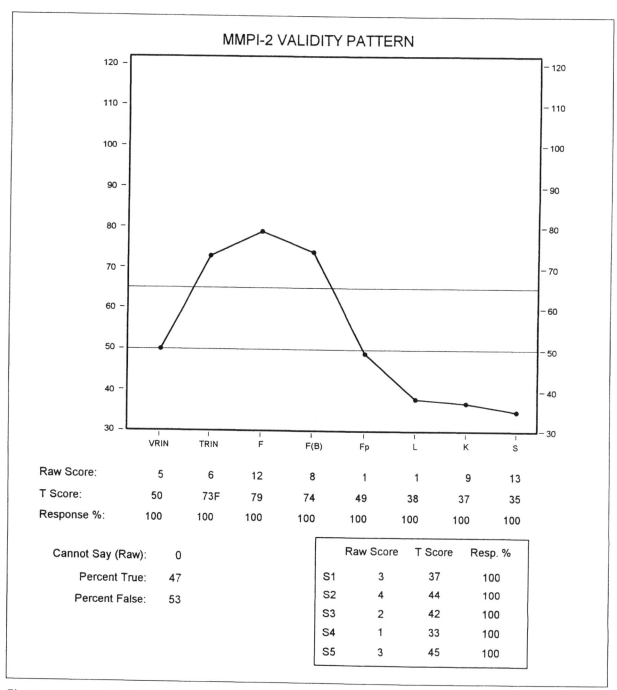

	VRIN	TRIN	F	F(B)	Fp	L	K	S
Raw Score:	5	6	12	8	1	1	9	13
T Score:	50	73F	79	74	49	38	37	35
Response %:	100	100	100	100	100	100	100	100

Cannot Say (Raw): 0

Percent True: 47

Percent False: 53

	Raw Score	T Score	Resp. %
S1	3	37	100
S2	4	44	100
S3	2	42	100
S4	1	33	100
S5	3	45	100

Figure 4. MMPI-2 validity scales profile for Case 4 (Elaine C.).

		(a)	(b)
Scale		**Level**	**Decision**
?	Cannot Say		
VRIN	Variable Response Inconsistency		
TRIN	True Response Inconsistency		
F	Infrequency		
F_b	Infrequency Back		
F_p	Infrequency Psychopathology		
L	Lie		
K	Defensiveness		
S	Superlative Self-Presentation		

(c) Given this validity profile configuration, are the other MMPI-2 scales interpretable? If not, why not?

_____

_____

_____

_____

_____

_____

_____

_____

_____

Case 5 (MMPI-A)

Case description: Carol J., a 15-year-old high school freshman, is being evaluated in a medical setting for problems centering on her school absences, complaints of fatigue, and inability to concentrate in school. She has been staying out late and her parents report that she is rebellious and hostile when they try to get her to go to school.

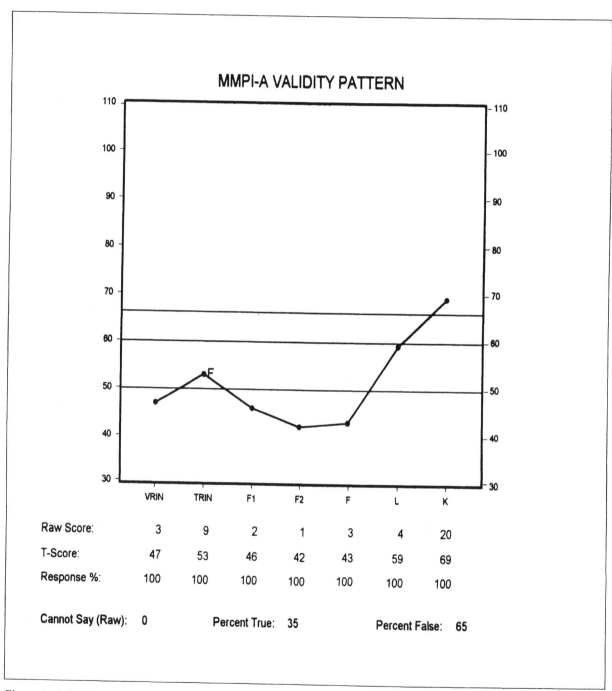

Figure 5. MMPI-A validity scales profile for Case 5 (Carol J.).

		(a)	(b)
Scale		**Level**	**Decision**
?	Cannot Say		
VRIN	Variable Response Inconsistency		
TRIN	True Response Inconsistency		
F_1	Infrequency 1		
F_2	Infrequency 2		
F	Infrequency		
L	Lie		
K	Defensiveness		

(c) Given this validity profile configuration, are the other MMPI-A scales interpretable? If not, why not?

_____

_____

_____

_____

_____

_____

_____

_____

Case 6 (MMPI-A)

Case description: Allie F., age 14, was referred to the school counselor for multiple psychological problems. She has been behaving in an antisocial and argumentative manner. She had numerous unexcused absences during a period when she had run away from home. She has been experiencing problems at home and at school since the beginning of the school year. She is failing in all her courses and shows no motivation to make up her work. Her parents reported to the school counselor that Allie does nothing they request of her and comes and goes as she pleases. She has been cited twice for curfew violation.

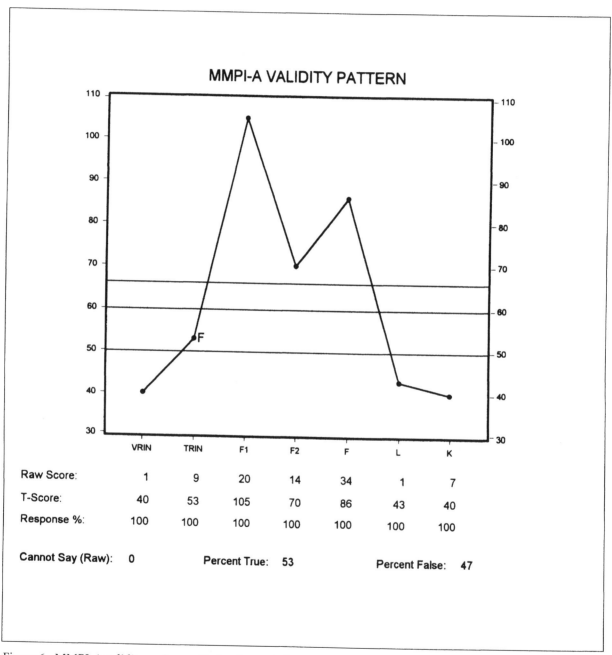

	VRIN	TRIN	F1	F2	F	L	K
Raw Score:	1	9	20	14	34	1	7
T-Score:	40	53	105	70	86	43	40
Response %:	100	100	100	100	100	100	100

Cannot Say (Raw): 0   Percent True: 53   Percent False: 47

Figure 6. MMPI-A validity scales profile for Case 6 (Allie F.).

		(a)	(b)
Scale		**Level**	**Decision**
?	Cannot Say		
VRIN	Variable Response Inconsistency		
TRIN	True Response Inconsistency		
F_1	Infrequency 1		
F_2	Infrequency 2		
F	Infrequency		
L	Lie		
K	Defensiveness		

(c) Given this validity profile configuration, are the other MMPI-A scales interpretable? If not, why not?

_____

_____

_____

_____

_____

_____

_____

_____

_____

Section 4

Interpreting the Clinical Scales

Several cases are provided in this section to give the beginning interpreter practice in profile interpretation. For each case a brief description of the client's history and problems is presented, along with the validity and clinical profiles. In the space provided, summarize the most likely profile interpretation.

Interpreting the clinical scales is relatively straightforward. Refer to the appropriate scale correlates section of the *Essentials* text for the relevant personality descriptors (see Chapter 4 for the MMPI-2 and Chapter 11 for the MMPI-A). Use single-scale descriptors if only one scale is elevated. Use two-point, three-point, or four-point codes for scales elevated at a T score greater than 65. For the MMPI-A, also interpret the scores that appear in the shaded area of the profile sheet. For example, if the profile is a single-scale spike such as a Pd score elevated at 71, then use the correlates for the Pd scale to summarize the empirical correlates for the profile. Develop sentences for your report using the correlate information. This section of the test report will most likely be the longest and most detailed of your MMPI-2 or MMPI-A report summary.

Case 7 (MMPI-2)

Case description: Kevin L., a 51-year-old married man, was evaluated as part of a work compensation claim. He worked for the postal service as a rural mail delivery person and claimed that he was unable to carry out his responsibilities because of a head injury he had suffered two years earlier when he fell on ice. He has not worked for more than two years, allegedly as a result of his injuries. His MMPI-2 validity scale pattern is given in Figure 7 and his clinical scale pattern in Figure 8.

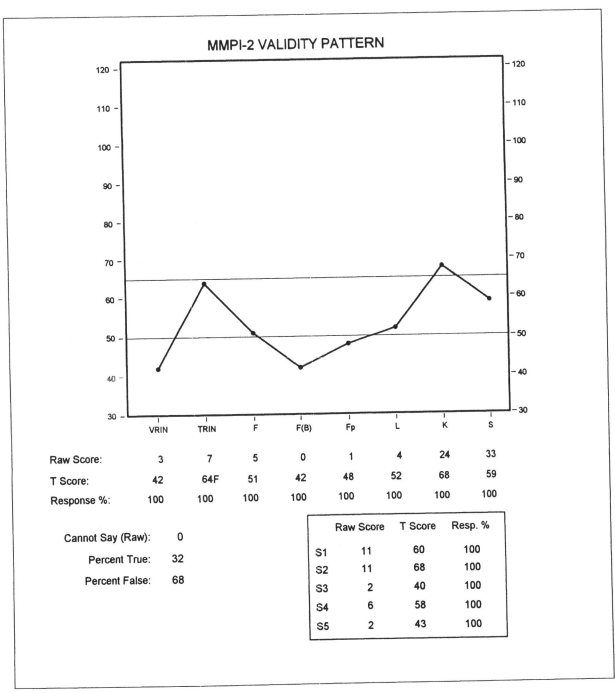

	VRIN	TRIN	F	F(B)	Fp	L	K	S
Raw Score:	3	7	5	0	1	4	24	33
T Score:	42	64F	51	42	48	52	68	59
Response %:	100	100	100	100	100	100	100	100

Cannot Say (Raw): 0

Percent True: 32

Percent False: 68

	Raw Score	T Score	Resp. %
S1	11	60	100
S2	11	68	100
S3	2	40	100
S4	6	58	100
S5	2	43	100

Figure 7. MMPI-2 validity scales profile for Case 7 (Kevin L.).

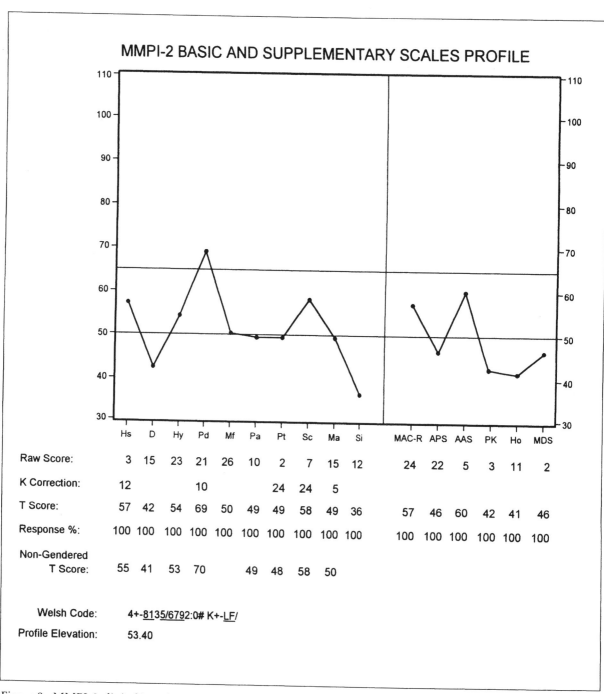

Figure 8. MMPI-2 clinical/supplementary scales profile for Case 7 (Kevin L.).

Summarize the information that might be obtained from the validity and clinical scales in this case.

Validity scale interpretation:

Clinical scale interpretation:

Case 8 (MMPI-2)

Case description: Joel P. is a 33-year-old applicant for a position as airline pilot for a major air carrier. He graduated from an aviation program at a large northeastern university with a degree in economics. He enlisted in the navy flight program and completed his training in the U.S. Navy. He flew carrier-based observation planes for one tour of duty. He plans to leave the navy as soon as he obtains employment with a major air carrier.

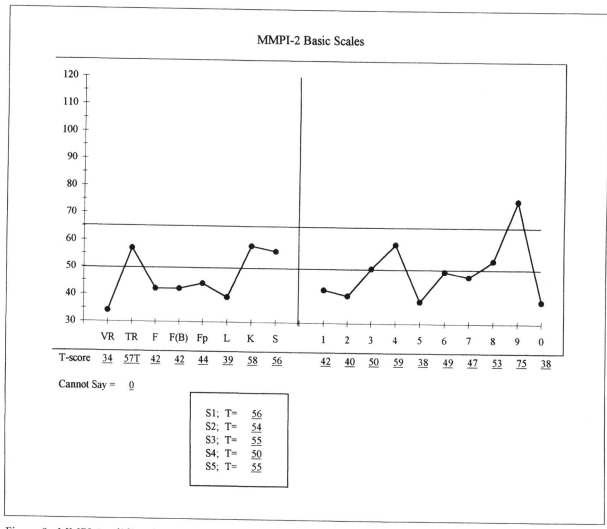

Figure 9. MMPI-2 validity/clinical scales profile for Case 8 (Joel P.).

Summarize the information that might be obtained from the validity and clinical scales in this case.

Validity scale interpretation:

Clinical scale interpretation:

Case 9 (MMPI-A)

Case description: Joe C., age 17, was referred to a counselor at the high school he was attending during his junior year. Joe reportedly had sixteen unexcused absences in the first three months of the school year and also has been reported to be defiant and verbally aggressive toward several of his teachers. His parents have indicated that he has also been rebellious with them and has stayed away from home for several days at a time. He was recommended for evaluation by his teachers and his parents.

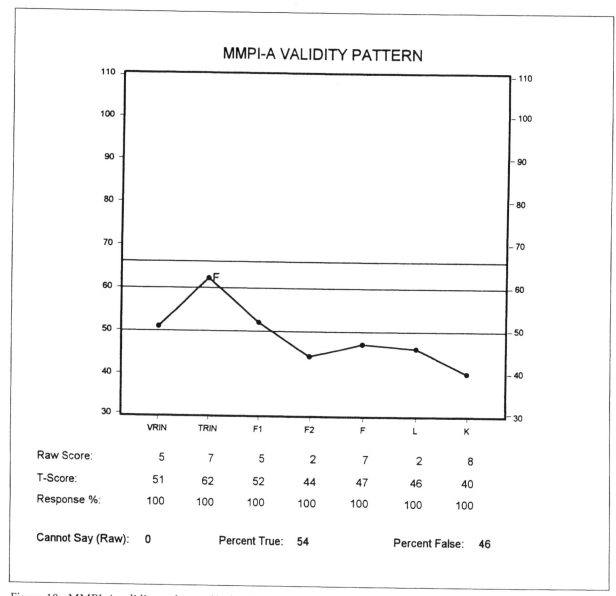

Figure 10. MMPI-A validity scales profile for Case 9 (Joe C.).

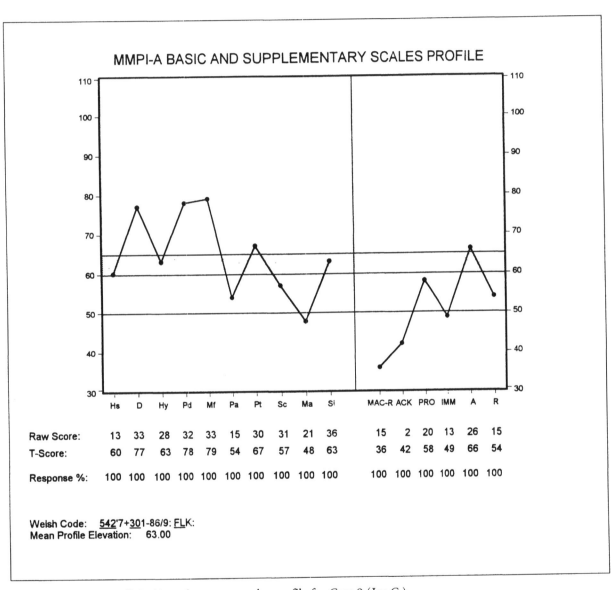

MMPI-A BASIC AND SUPPLEMENTARY SCALES PROFILE

	Hs	D	Hy	Pd	Mf	Pa	Pt	Sc	Ma	Si		MAC-R	ACK	PRO	IMM	A	R
Raw Score:	13	33	28	32	33	15	30	31	21	36		15	2	20	13	26	15
T-Score:	60	77	63	78	79	54	67	57	48	63		36	42	58	49	66	54
Response %:	100	100	100	100	100	100	100	100	100	100		100	100	100	100	100	100

Welsh Code: 542'7+301-86/9: FLK:
Mean Profile Elevation: 63.00

Figure 11. MMPI-A clinical/supplementary scales profile for Case 9 (Joe C.).

Summarize the information that might be obtained from the validity and clinical scales in this case.

Validity scale interpretation:

Clinical scale interpretation:

Case 10 (MMPI-A)

Case description: Janet C., a 15-year-old girl in ninth grade, was recently suspended from school because of her antagonistic attitudes, for lying to her teacher about her unexcused absences, and for bringing drugs (amphetamines) onto the school premises. Her academic performance has been poor for the past two years.

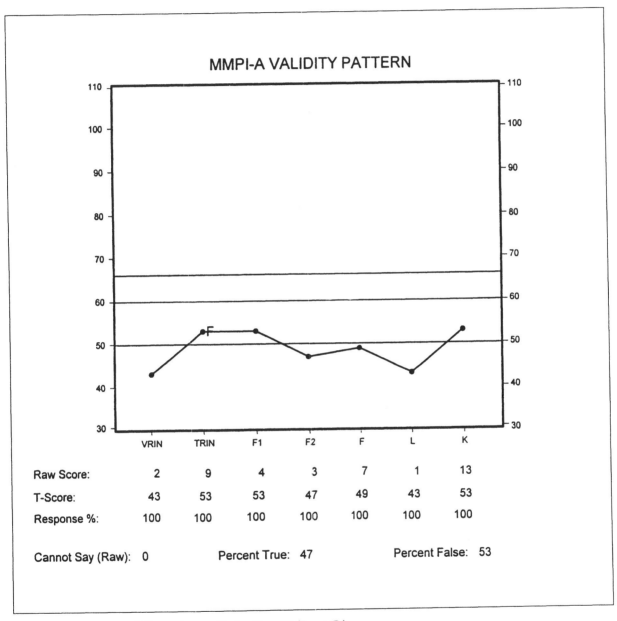

	VRIN	TRIN	F1	F2	F	L	K
Raw Score:	2	9	4	3	7	1	13
T-Score:	43	53	53	47	49	43	53
Response %:	100	100	100	100	100	100	100

Cannot Say (Raw): 0   Percent True: 47   Percent False: 53

Figure 12. MMPI-A validity scales profile for Case 10 (Janet C.).

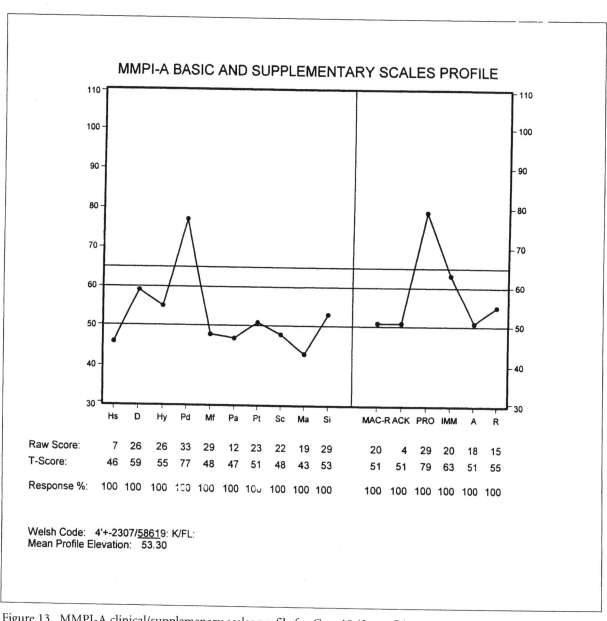

Figure 13. MMPI-A clinical/supplemenary scales profile for Case 10 (Janet C.).

Summarize the information that might be obtained from the validity and clinical scales in this case.

Validity scale interpretation:

Clinical scale interpretation:

Section 5

Interpreting the Content Scales

Interpreting the MMPI-2 and MMPI-A content scales requires a strategy different from interpreting the clinical scales. Refer to Chapter 6 in *Essentials* for a discussion of the MMPI-2 content scales and chapter 12 for the MMPI-A content scales. The content scales provide summary scores for various content themes the client has endorsed. The interpreter develops a paragraph summarizing the content of the highest scale elevations in the client's profile. For example, if one content scale is elevated above a T score of 65 (e.g., the ANX scale), then the paragraph would summarize the item contents that make up that scale as the main themes the client is presenting in his or her item endorsements.

Case 11 (MMPI-2)

Case description: Ann B., a 30-year-old divorced mother of three, is currently embroiled in a custody dispute. She and her former husband of ten years experienced marital problems for most of their marriage. Ann is a recovering substance abuser and is currently unemployed. She has temporary custody of their three children, but her ex-husband (who has remarried) is seeking full custody. The MMPI-2 was administered to her as part of the custody proceedings.

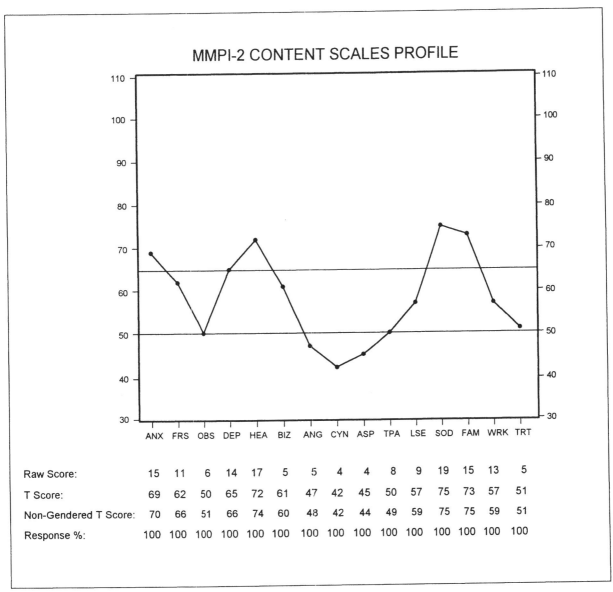

Figure 14. MMPI-2 content scales profile for Case 11 (Ann C.).

Through the MMPI-2 content scale, describe how Ann is describing herself and her current problem situation.

Content scale summary:

Case 12 (MMPI-2)

Case description: Charlie S., age 28, was arrested after a hit and run accident. He had had an intense disagreement with his wife, then left their apartment in a rage and, within a mile, hit a pedestrian (who happened to be a journalist) in a crosswalk. The journalist was hospitalized in critical condition. The police tracked Charlie's vehicle and arrested him the following day. In all likelihood Charlie was under the influence of alcohol at the time of the accident; he was not found to be inebriated at the time of his arrest. He was charged with careless/reckless driving and leaving the scene of an accident. Charlie had an arrest for spousal abuse within the past two years.

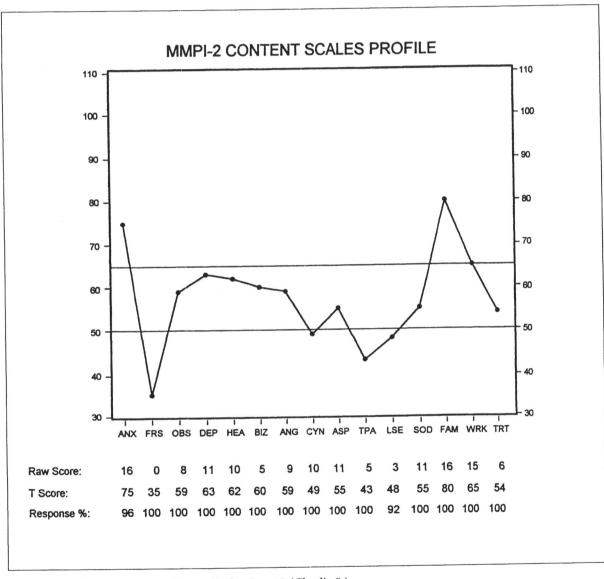

Figure 15. MMPI-2 content scales profile for Case 12 (Charlie S.).

Content scale summary.

54

Case 13 (MMPI-A)

Case description: Jenny A., a 17-year-old high school junior, was evaluated by the school psychologist following a number of excused absences from school. Jenny had been an average student through her sophomore year, but her school performance gradually deteriorated this past year. Three months before she was referred for evaluation, she was arrested with several other juveniles after a "kegger" party got out of hand. Jenny's parents have been divorced for two years and there is a great deal of family tension. Jenny is currently living with her mother; her father lives across town with his new wife and her two preteen children. Her father is not involved with Jenny at this point, considering her "grown up." Jenny's mother works evenings and weekends and often does not know where Jenny is.

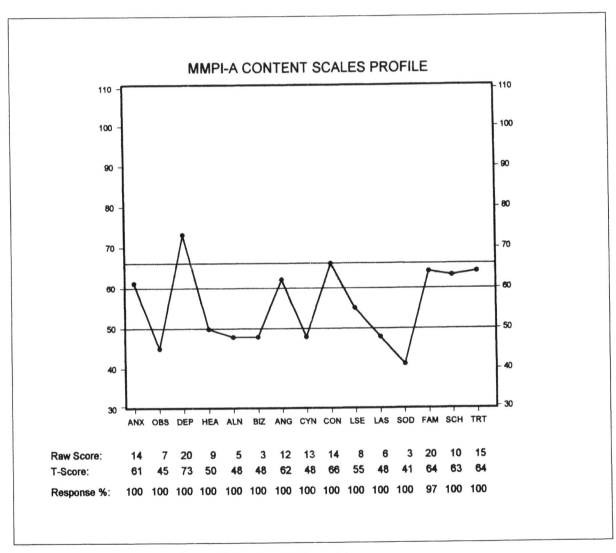

Figure 16. MMPI-A content scales profile for Case 13 (Jenny A.).

Content Scale summary:

Case 14 (MMPI-A)

Case description: Del B., age 15, is currently in ninth grade after having failed the same grade the previous year. He has become very uninvolved in school. He belongs to a juvenile gang that prides itself on skipping school, wearing flashy starter jackets, and hanging out at a large shopping mall. Although his parents have tried to modify his behavior, they have not been able to rein him in. Del has been arrested twice during the past six months, once for shoplifting and the second time for underage drinking (and possession of an open bottle of alcohol in a friend's car). Although he has been a marginal student for several years (in part the result of low ability), his performance in school over the past two years has gotten worse. He longs to be 16, so he can quit school. Most of his friends have already done so.

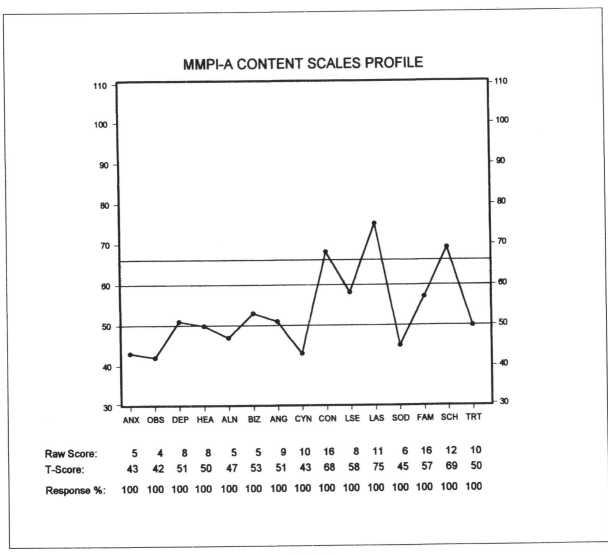

Figure 17. MMPI-A content scales profile for Case 14 (Del B.).

Content scale summary:

Section 6

Interpreting Supplementary or Special Scales

The MMPI-2 and MMPI-A supplementary scales assess characteristics or problems not sufficiently addressed by the clinical or content scales. The most widely used of these measures are the three scales dealing with problems of addiction.

MMPI-2	**MMPI-A**
A (Anxiety) Scale (Welsh)	Same
R (Repression) Scale (Welsh)	Same
MacAndrew Alcoholism-Revised Scale (MAC-R)	Same
Addiction Proneness Scale (APS)	Alcohol/Drug Problem Proneness (PRO)
Addiction Admission Scale (AAS)	Alcohol/Drug Problem Acknowledgment (ACK)
Marital Distress Scale (MDS)	Immaturity (IMM)
Hostility Scale (Ho)	
Post-Traumatic Stress Disorder Scale (Pk)	

The section of the MMPI-2 or MMPI-A report focusing on the interpretation of elevated supplementary scales usually follows the empirical descriptions of the clinical scales and the summary of the elevated content scales. It is usually brief, a sentence or two highlighting the prominent scale elevations. For example, if the AAS scale is the only supplementary scale elevated (a T score above 60) for a male client, then a statement such as the following might be appropriate: "His acknowledgment of extensive alcohol or drug use should be evaluated further. It is likely that he has a substance abuse problem."

Case 15 (MMPI-2)

Case description: Sue T., a 39-year-old separated woman with two teenage children, was prompted to seek a psychological evaluation by both her husband and her attorney. She recently had a second DWI arrest in as many months. She is awaiting trial for the second charge and is likely to lose her driver's license for a minimum of one year. She and her husband have been separated for six months and she has temporary custody of the two children. Her husband, who is seeking the divorce, plans to remarry, although he is uncertain about whether he will seek custody of the children. Sue has also been having difficulty with her job—she is currently on probation—as a result of missing a lot of work over the past few months. She has apparently recognized to some extent that she has a drinking problem and has willingly sought the evaluation.

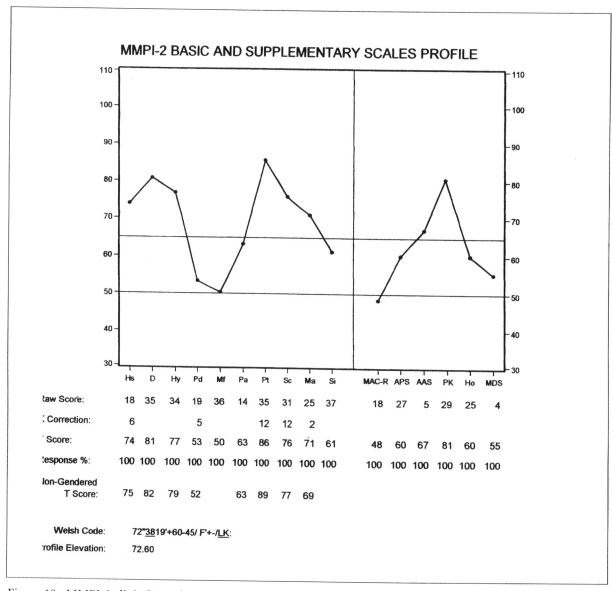

Figure 18. MMPI-2 clinical/supplementary scales profile for Case 15 (Sue T.).

Summary of supplementary scale performance:

Case 16 (MMPI-2)

Case description: Robert L., a 40-year-old divorced hotel assistant manager, was evaluated at the request of his employer because of recent incidents involving alcohol. Robert was found to have been drinking on the job and has been performing below expectation. The manager of the hotel services corporation (out of respect for Robert's long service with the company) referred him for substance abuse evaluation rather than terminating his employment. Robert only reluctantly consented to the evaluation. As noted by his MMPI-2 clinical score elevation on Pa, Robert was generally suspicious and tended to deny any responsibility for his problems.

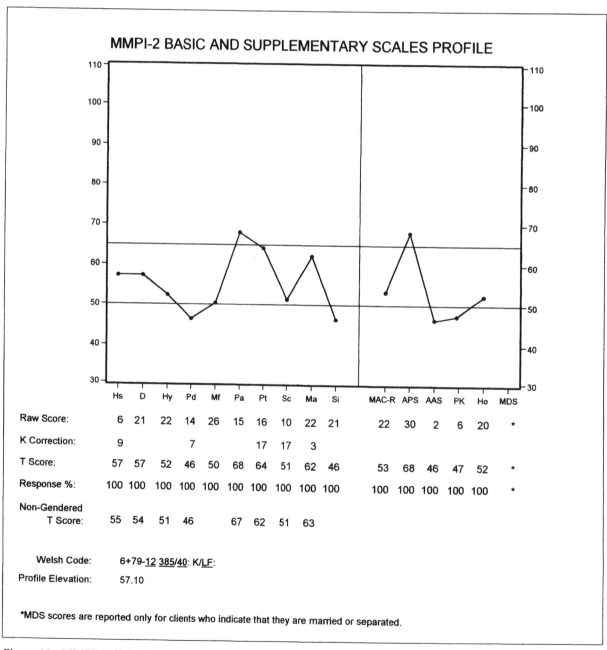

Figure 19. MMPI-2 clinical/supplementary scales profile for Case 16 (Robert L.).

Summary of supplementary scale performance:

Case 17 (MMPI-A)

Case description: Gina L. is a white 18-year-old high school senior living at home with her parents and a younger sister. Her older brother and sister live elsewhere. Gina was admitted to an inpatient alcohol and drug treatment program following two suicide attempts. She had also had two recent alcohol-related arrests (for driving while intoxicated and drinking under age). The admitting clinician suggested that depression, generalized anxiety disorder, and alcohol or other drug problems be considered in her problem picture. She was given antidepressant medication at discharge. Multiple symptoms of anxiety and depression were noted among her current problems. Both her father and brother had histories of alcohol and drug problems (for additional information, see Butcher & Williams, 1992).

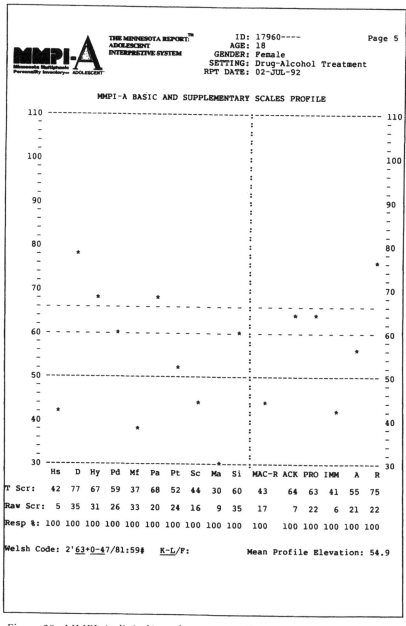

Figure 20. MMPI-A clinical/supplementary scales profile for Case 17 (Gina L.).

Summary of supplementary scale performance:

Case 18 (MMPI-A)

Case description: Brenda, a 16-year-old Caucasian girl, was seen in an outpatient diagnostic evaluation. She had been placed in the custody of the county children services because of severe parental conflict. She was evaluated because of her depression and suicide attempts. She complained of low mood and pessimism about the future. She also reported being anxious and having a large number of somatic complaints.

Brenda first attempted suicide in fifth grade at age 11, when she overdosed on Tylenol and cut her wrists. She reported that she did this because of her overcontrolling mother and because of extreme family conflict. At that time she was admitted to an inpatient facility for three weeks. For the past few years Brenda has lived with her father, but supervision of her has been lax. She started dating a 23-year-old man during this period. She also used marijuana and alcohol. At the time of the evaluation she was living with a friend and had dropped out of high school.

In the psychological/psychiatric examination she received a diagnosis of Major Depressive Disorder, without psychotic features; Conduct Disorder; Parent-Child Relational Disorder; and Learning Disorder.

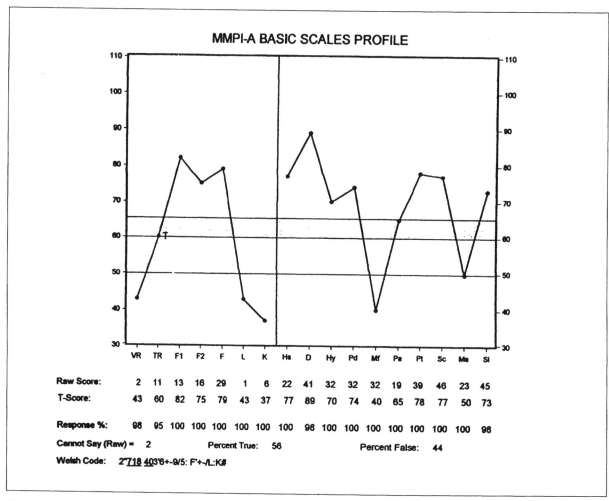

Figure 21. MMPI-A validity/clinical scales profile (with supplementary scale scores reported on next page) for Case 18 (Brenda)

Supplementary Score Report

Supplementary Scale	Raw Score	T Score	Response %
MacAndrew Alcoholism-Revised (MAC-R)	26	65	100
Alcohol/Drug Problem Acknowledgment (ACK)	5	56	100
Alcohol/Drug Problem Proneness (PRO)	31	84	100
Immaturity Scale (IMM)	26	73	98
Anxiety (A)	27	63	100
Repression (R)	19	66	100

Summary of supplementary scale performance:

Section 7

Exercise: Profile Interpretation

This section gives the beginning MMPI-2 and MMPI-A interpreter practice in interpreting the test with a variety of clients to arrive at general personality descriptions from the various sources of information in the inventories. To give a perspective on the case, profiles from several applied settings will be provided, along with information about the testing situation, the assessment problem, and the individual's social history and background characteristics.

The steps in developing a clinical interpretation are as follows.

1. Ensure that all the validity scales are in the interpretable range. If any of the validity scales are uninterpretable, the clinical and content scales should not be interpreted.

2. Examine the *profile code* to determine the most elevated scales in the profile. Interpret scale elevations in terms of the distance of the T score from the mean of the normative sample (T = 50).

3. Determine if any clinical scales are elevated in the interpretable range—for example, with a T score equal to or greater than 65. In the range of T = 60 (one standard deviation) to T = 64, the personality correlates are not considered to apply to the individual. At or above a T of 65, apply all correlates of the scale as indicated.

4. Take into consideration *profile definition* to determine the most salient pattern to interpret, that is, the extent to which a high point score is elevated above the next highest scale in the profile.

5. Use the "specified code type" (e.g., one-, two-, three-, or four-point code) to search the empirical scale literature to obtain relevant scale correlates.

6. The higher a scale score, the more like the criterion group the patient is assumed to be and the more defining patient characteristics he or she is likely to have.

7. Examine the Harris-Lingoes subscale elevations of the elevated clinical scales to guide you in ordering the code-type correlates.

8. Evaluate important content themes as represented through significant elevations of the content scales. Integrate important content themes into the summary.

9. Evaluate possible problems reflected in the supplementary scale elevations.

In the cases of this section, write a summary for each of these categories: profile validity; symptomatic behavior; interpersonal behavior; diagnostic considerations; and treatment considerations. After you have completed this exercise, you may check your interpretation against the interpretation generated by the computer.

The computer-based narrative reports are included to give the beginning interpreter an example of how particular profiles are interpreted by computer. Most of the information contained in the computer-generated reports is available in the research literature on the instruments. The beginning interpreter should keep these points in mind:

- A computer-based interpretation program is simply an electronic textbook that looks up relevant descriptors.
- The narrative statements provided are hypotheses, not confirmed facts, about the client.
- The statements are guides to interpreting a particular pattern, not considered the "end all" in interpretation.
- The psychologist using a computer-generated report should know the MMPI-2 or MMPI-A interpretive literature and should verify whether the pattern of information generated is appropriate for the case.
- Computer-based reports can be valuable in teaching profile interpretation because they likely provide the most objective, replicable information about the pattern being interpreted.

Case 19 (MMPI-2)

Case description: Tamara P., a 31-year-old African-American prostitute, was recently arrested (for the twenty-first time) for drug possession and prostitution. A year ago she was convicted of carrying a weapon and for possession of a large quantity of an illegal drug (second offense), and she spent eight months in jail. The present evaluation was recommended as a pre-sentencing psychological study because she is now facing a mandatory nine-year prison term if she is found guilty of the current charges. The judge ordered the evaluation to determine the extent to which mental health factors and substance abuse were central to her problems.

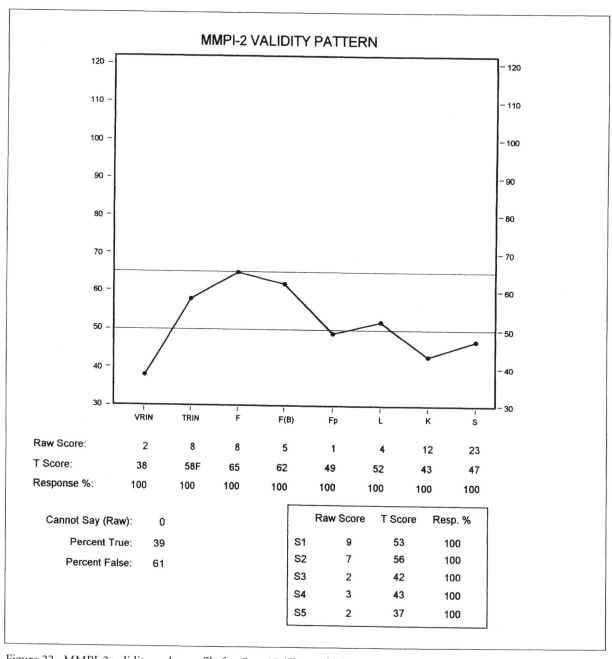

Figure 22. MMPI-2 validity scales profile for Case 19 (Tamaral P.).

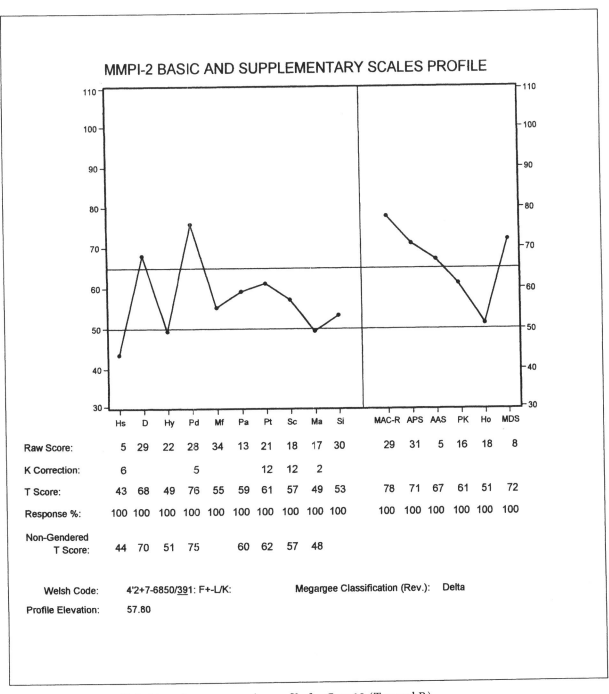

MMPI-2 BASIC AND SUPPLEMENTARY SCALES PROFILE

	Hs	D	Hy	Pd	Mf	Pa	Pt	Sc	Ma	Si		MAC-R	APS	AAS	PK	Ho	MDS
Raw Score:	5	29	22	28	34	13	21	18	17	30		29	31	5	16	18	8
K Correction:	6			5			12	12	2								
T Score:	43	68	49	76	55	59	61	57	49	53		78	71	67	61	51	72
Response %:	100	100	100	100	100	100	100	100	100	100		100	100	100	100	100	100
Non-Gendered T Score:	44	70	51	75		60	62	57	48								

Welsh Code: 4'2+7-6850/391: F+-L/K: Megargee Classification (Rev.):   Delta

Profile Elevation: 57.80

Figure 23. MMPI-2 clinical/supplementary scales profile for Case 19 (Tamaral P.).

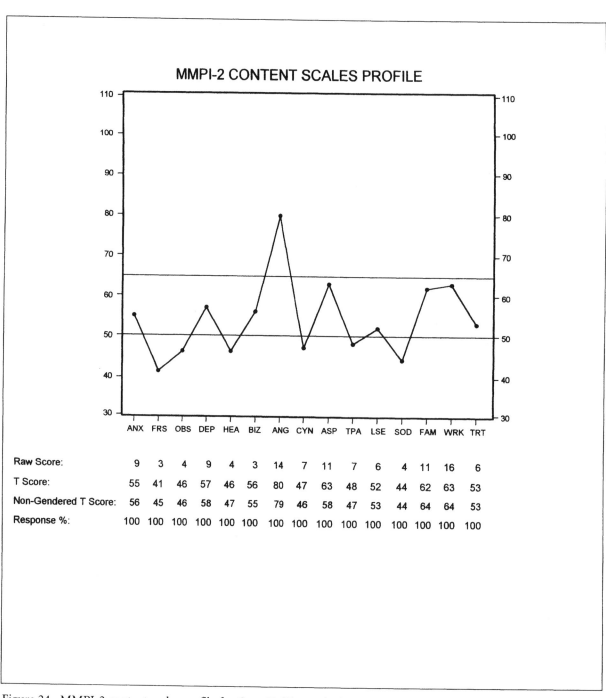

Figure 24. MMPI-2 content scales profile for Case 19 (Tamaral P.).

Profile validity:

Symptomatic behavior:

Interpersonal behavior:

Diagnostic considerations:

Treatment considerations:

Case 20 (MMPI-A)

This case was adapted from J. N. Butcher et al., *International Case Studies on the MMPI-A: An Objective Approach* (Minneapolis: University of Minnesota Press, 2000).

Case description: Adriana was born on December 23, 1981, and is an only child. Her parents divorced when she was three years old. At present, she lives with her mother and stepfather. Her mother remarried when Adriana was five.

Adriana was referred to therapy because she became violent toward her mother and broke her mother's arm. She has reportedly been demonstrating many aberrant behaviors: she is very aggressive, has bulimia, and has problems with drugs and alcohol. Her mother has also been in therapy for many years and has been admitted to a hospital several times for depression and constant insomnia. Her biological father has always been an alcoholic. He always drank and was very abusive toward Adriana's mother. This was the reason her parents divorced. The father married again and had another daughter. He has continued to drink until recently.

When Adriana was 15, she displayed many symptoms of bulimia. She would eat in excess and then would vomit immediately afterward. More recently, she has been experiencing a voluntary or reflective bulimia attack at least twice a week.

At 16, Adriana started drinking and smoking—about three glasses of rum and coke and two bottles of beer over a weekend. She acknowledged that she gets drunk easily and becomes aggressive at times. She also started using marijuana at public parks, but she stopped four months ago. She's been in trouble with the police and she has been accused of being a small drug dealer. She is currently under police scrutiny. She currently smokes four cigarettes per day.

She reportedly has been experiencing a great deal of difficulty at school. She has reported problems with some of her classes, especially math, chemistry, and physics. Her school failures required that she repeat seventh grade. She was expelled from school for aggressiveness and smoking. She was in two middle schools. She is currently in eleventh grade and performing poorly.

Her relationship with her father is reportedly not particularly problematic, in part because there is not much communication between them. Most of the time her father has been "borracho" (drunk) and continues to act aggressively toward Adriana's mother—often calling her names. Adriana lives with her father only sporadically and he has never been very nice to her. He calls her names and insults her, but has never hurt her physically. Recently, her father has tried to change his behavior; he stopped drinking twenty months ago, saying he wants to have a good relationship with his daughter and his ex-wife. Adriana's relationship with her stepfather seems to be better; she seems to respect him more. He's very strict with her and always insists on her being truthful. He reprimands her when she drinks, smokes, or behaves inappropriately.

Her current relationship with her mother is not particularly good. They are always arguing about Adriana's behavior, especially relating to drinking and bulimia. In spite of that, Adriana says that she loves her mother and she doesn't mean to hurt her—it is just that sometimes she loses control. She doesn't remember breaking her mother's arm: she says she was drunk.

She promises her mother that she will change but never fulfills her promise because she feels her mother is overcontrolling. She said the bulimia started as a way to get her mother's attention. She also caused problems with her mother because she wouldn't clean up the mess after vomiting that she would initiate by putting her finger down her throat. When her mother wouldn't let her go out with her friends, she would tell her that she was going to kill herself and that it would be her mother's fault.

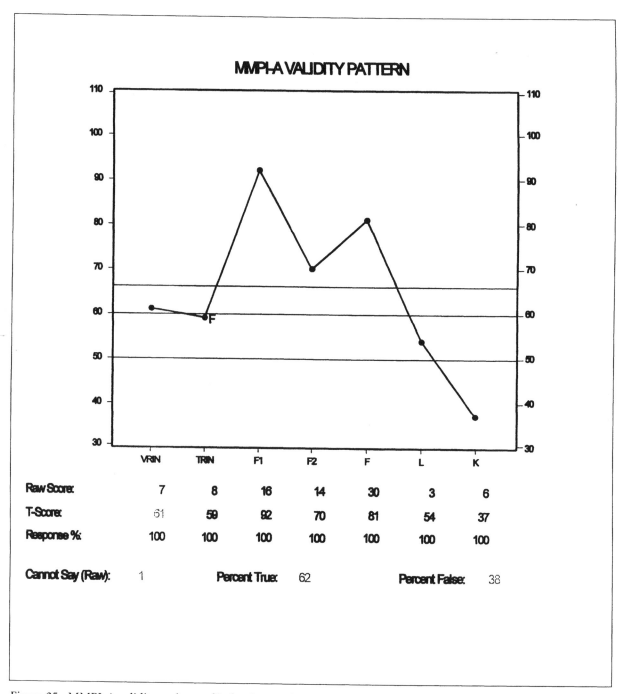

Figure 25. MMPI-A validity scales profile for Case 20 (Adriana).

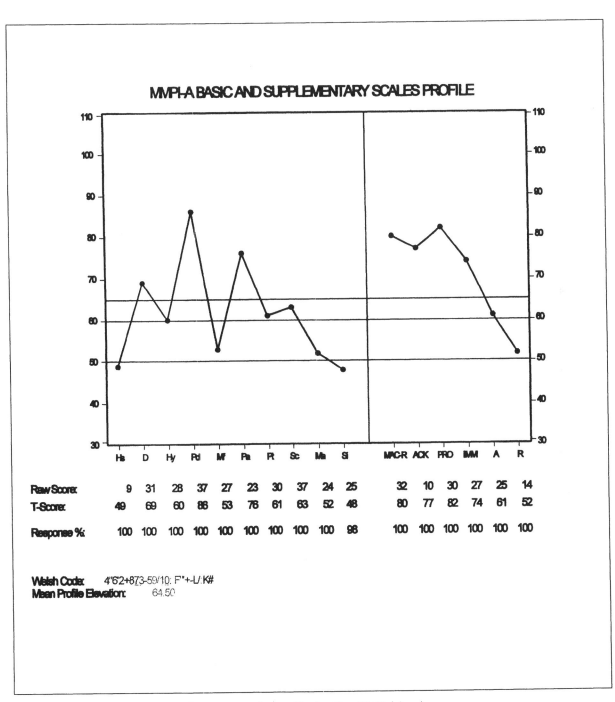

MMPI-A BASIC AND SUPPLEMENTARY SCALES PROFILE

	Hs	D	Hy	Pd	Mf	Pa	Pt	Sc	Ma	Si		MAC-R	ACK	PRO	IMM	A	R
Raw Score:	9	31	28	37	27	23	30	37	24	25		32	10	30	27	25	14
T-Score:	49	69	60	86	53	76	61	63	52	48		80	77	82	74	61	52
Response %:	100	100	100	100	100	100	100	100	100	98		100	100	100	100	100	100

Welsh Code: 4'6'2+8?3-59/10: F"+-L/:K#
Mean Profile Elevation: 64.50

Figure 26. MMPI-A clinical/supplementary scales profile for Case 20 (Adriana).

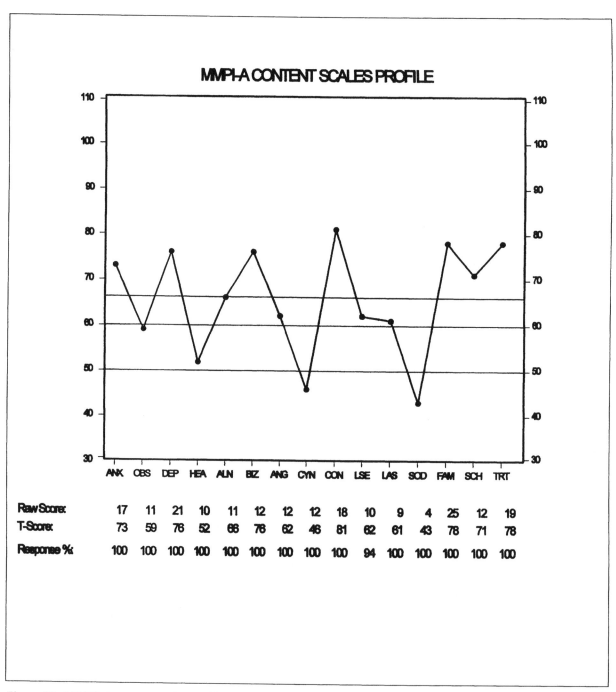

Figure 27. MMPI-A content scales profile for Case 20 (Adriana).

78

Profile validity:

Symptomatic behavior:

Interpersonal relations:

Behavioral stability:

Diagnostic considerations:

Treatment considerations:

Glossary

This glossary was designed as a quick reference to the most frequently used technical terms and abbreviations relating to the MMPI-2 and MMPI-A. It is not a comprehensive psychometric dictionary but simply a handy reference tool. Note that all content scales unique to the MMPI-A are listed in this glossary (for example, A-aln); content scales that appear in both the MMPI-2 and MMPI-A are listed by their MMPI-2 abbreviated and full names (for example, ANX; the MMPI-A scale is A-anx).

A scale or Anxiety (Welsh). A factor analytic scale that defines the first major factor in the MMPI-2 and MMPI-A item pools—anxiety or general maladjustment.

ACK or Alcohol/Drug Problem Acknowledgment scale. An MMPI-A scale developed to assess whether an adolescent is acknowledging using or abusing alcohol or drugs.

A-aln or Adolescent-Alienation scale. An MMPI-A content scale measuring the extent to which an adolescent feels distanced from other people.

AAS or Addiction Admission scale. A rationally derived MMPI-2 scale assessing a client's experience with alcohol or drugs. A high score on this scale indicates that the client has endorsed a significant number of substance abuse problems.

A-con or Adolescent–Conduct Problems scale. An MMPI-A content scale assessing problems of conduct disorder.

Acting out. A term usually used within a psychoanalytic or psychodynamic framework to denote a defense in which individuals express painful or "unacceptable" emotions through behavior as a way to keep the emotions unconscious (or out of awareness).

Actuarial prediction. The application of probability statistics to human behavior, as in insurance mortality tables.

Acute Post-Traumatic Stress Disorder (PTSD). A disorder in which symptoms develop within six months of an extremely stressful or traumatic experience.

Adaptive testing. A method of test administration that uses the rapid computational capability of the computer to administer a different set of items for each person depending on the person's responses to previous items.

Addiction Proneness. A theoretical construct concerning the likelihood that an individual will develop substance abuse disorders.

Affect. The experience of feelings or emotion.

A-las or Low Aspirations scale. An MMPI-A content scale assessing poor attitudes toward achievement and being a success in life. Although related to the School Problems scale, its content is more general, including dislike of sports and nonschool activities.

ANG or Anger scale. An MMPI-2 Content scale.

Antisocial personality. Personality disorder involving a marked lack of ethical or moral development.

ANX or Anxiety scale. An MMPI-2 content scale.

APS or Addiction Proneness scale. An empirically derived MMPI-2 scale assessing the likelihood that an individual has a substance-abuse problem.

A-sch or School Problems scale. An MMPI-A content scale that addressess school-related problems.

ASP or Antisocial Practices scale. An MMPI-2 content scale.

Automated assessment. Psychological test interpretation by computer or other mechanical procedure.

Bimodal distribution. A statistical term indicating a distribution in which two values (or scores) are tied in terms of being most frequent; the distribution thus has two modes.

BIZ or Bizarre Mentation scale. An MMPI-2 content scale.

(?) Cannot Say. The total number of unanswered items on the MMPI-2 or MMPI-A, serving as an indicator of test validity.

Central tendency. A statistical term indicating the average. Measures of central tendency include the mean, the median, and the mode (see **Mean, Median, Mode**).

Clinical scale. Items that have been grouped into scales according to empirical validation methods—that is, items comprising the scale were found to significantly discriminate a criterion group of patients from a normal reference sample. A particular empirical scale (for example, to measure depression) is interpreted by referring to empirical correlates (extra-test behaviors) established through validation research.

Code type. A summary index of the most prominent MMPI-2 scales. A one-point code type, or spike, has one prominent scale; a two-point code type consists of two scales elevated in the interpretable range.

Content scale. A psychometric measure developed by rational-empirical methods to assess homogeneous content themes in the MMPI-2 and MMPI-A.

Correlation coefficient. A statistic indicating the degree to which two variables are related (whether they co-vary or vary together). The coefficient falls somewhere on a continuum from -1 (perfectly negatively correlated) to 0 (no relationship whatsoever) to 1 (perfectly positively correlated).

Criterion group. A sample of persons, such as depressed clinical patients or persons with a substance abuse disorder, who are assumed to have common characteristics. This group is contrasted with a group of normal individuals to develop empirical scales by selecting items that differentiate the criterion group from normals.

Critical items. Items that serve as possible indicators of clinical or personality problems, for example, "suicidal ideation" or "anger control problems."

Cut-off score. A somewhat arbitrary point in an MMPI-2 or MMPI-A scale distribution at which a particular interpretation or decision is made.

CYN or Cynicism scale. An MMPI-2 content scale.

D or Depression scale (Scale 2). An MMPI-2 and MMPI-A clinical scale.

Decompensation. The deterioration of an individual's personality, condition, or functioning.

Defense mechanisms. A term used to describe a process, usually within a psychoanalytic or psychodynamic framework, by which an individual wards off awareness of unpleasant, frightening, or anxiety-inducing thoughts or experiences; these strategies are carried out on an unconscious level (i.e., the individual is not aware of them).

Delusion. A false belief or one that is not consistent with reality and is rigidly maintained in spite of strong evidence to the contrary.

Dementia. Substantial loss of mental or cognitive abilities.

DEP or Depression scale. An MMPI-2 content scale.

Descriptive statistics. Statistics that apply only to cases that have actually been counted or otherwise measured; no attempt is made to draw inferences about populations beyond what has actually been counted or measured.

Diagnostic and Statistical Manual of Mental Disorders (DSM). A classification system by which mental, emotional, and behavioral disorders have been defined, described, and labeled, published by the American Psychiatric Association; the first edition appeared in 1952. After the second edition in 1968, a multiaxial system of diagnosis was developed (American Psychiatric Association, 1980, 1987): Axis I presents clinical disorders or syndromes (as well as treatment issues that do not concern mental disorders and some supplementary codes); Axis II presents personality and developmental disorders; Axis III presents physical disorders; Axis IV indicates the level of psychosocial stress; and Axis V indicates the best level of functioning the individual has experienced during the past year.

Empirical correlates. The relationships between MMPI-2 or MMPI-A scores and observed external behavior are described as "empirical correlates" for a given scale. Empirical correlates for the scales are symptoms, behaviors, and attitudes that have been found present in patients with prominent elevations on a given scale or scales.

Empirical scale construction. A scale construction strategy by which items are selected for a scale if they significantly discriminate two clearly defined groups from each other, such as "depressive patients" and "normals." Item selection is based on empirical or external validation methods.

F scale. An MMPI-2 and MMPI-A validity scale measuring "infrequency" or exaggeration of symptoms.

F_b scale. An MMPI-2 validity scale created to measure exaggeration of symptoms toward the end of the MMPI-2 booklet.

F_p scale. An MMPI-2 validity scale developed to measure exaggeration of symptoms or infrequent responses within a psychiatric sample.

F_1 scale. An MMPI-A validity scale measuring infrequent responses or exaggeration of symptoms in the first part of the MMPI-A booklet.

F_2 scale. An MMPI-A validity scale measuring exaggeration of symptoms or infrequent responses toward the end of the MMPI-A booklet.

Factor analysis. A statistical technique employed in research to reduce a large array of measurements or data to more concise and fundamental dimensions.

Fake-bad profile. A validity scale profile indicating that the test-taker has made an effort to distort MMPI-2 results by claiming mental health symptoms he or she does not have. The fake-bad profile usually has an extremely elevated F, F_b, or F_p pattern and relatively low scores on L, K, and S.

Fake-good profile. A validity scale profile indicating that the test-taker made an effort to distort MMPI-2 results by presenting an overly favorable self-view or a "good impression." The fake-good profile usually has an extremely elevated pattern of L, K, and S scales and relatively low scores on F, F_b, and Fp.

False negative. An error in assessment in which a test falsely indicates that the individual does not have a particular condition (that the test was designed to identify) when in fact the person does have the condition (see **False positive, Sensitivity,** and **Specificity**).

False positive. An assessment error in which a test falsely indicates that an individual has a particular condition (that the test was designed to identify) when in fact the person does not have the condition (see **False negative, Sensitivity,** and **Specificity**).

FAM or Family Problems scale. An MMPI-2 content scale.

Floating profile. A term indicating that T scores on all ten standard scales are above 65.

FRS or Fears scale. An MMPI-2 content scale.

Functional disorder. A form of psychopathological distress or dysfunction for which a physiological cause is neither known nor presumed.

Functional psychoses. Severe mental disorders attributed primarily to psychological causes such as stress.

HEA or Health Concerns scale. An MMPI-2 content scale.

Ho or Hostility scale. An MMPI-2 scale assessing interpersonal problems and self-reported hostile, aggressive behavior.

Hs or Hypochondriasis scale (scale 1). An MMPI-2 and MMPI-A clinical scale measuring somatic concerns (see Chapter 2 and Appendix D).

Hy or Hysteria scale (scale 3). An MMPI-2 and MMPI-A clinical scale measuring physical complaints and denial of problems.

Incidence. The rate at which a phenomenon occurs.

Inferential statistics. Statistical techniques allowing inferences to be made about a larger population based on a presumably representative sample or subset of that population.

K correction. Fractions of the K-scale score added to several MMPI-2 clinical scales to correct for defensiveness.

K scale. An MMPI-2 and MMPI-A validity scale measuring test defensiveness.

Kurtosis. A statistical term describing the degree to which scores or measurements are clustered closely around or are spread far from the mean.

L or Lie scale. An MMPI-2 and MMPI-A validity scale measuring the tendency to claim excessive virtue.

Linear T scores. A statistical term (see **T scores**) in which the mean of the distribution is 50 and the standard deviation is 10; the type of score used in the original MMPI. The linear T distribution formula is:

$$T = 50 + [10(X - MEAN)] / SD$$

where

X = each raw score that could potentially be obtained for a given MMPI scale

MEAN = the mean raw score among subjects for that scale

SD = the standard deviation among subjects for that scale

LSE or Low Self-Esteem scale. An MMPI-2 content scale.

Ma or Hypomania scale (scale 9). A clinical scale on the MMPI-2 and MMPI-A measuring behavioral features of manic and manic-depressive episodes (see Chapter 2 and Appendix D).

MAC-R or MacAndrew-Revised scale. An empirically derived scale assessing addiction proneness, revised for inclusion on the MMPI-2 and MMPI-A.

MDS or Marital Distress scale. An empirically derived MMPI-2 scale assessing relationship or marital problems.

Mean. An arithmetical average in which the scores (or other numbers) are added and the resulting sum is then divided by the number of scores.

Median. A statistical term indicating the score or measurement that divides all the scores or measurements into two equal groups, those falling below the median and those falling above the median.

Megargee Offender Classification System. A classification system designed to group the MMPI-2 profiles of felons into personality clusters.

Mf or Masculinity-Femininity scale (scale 5). A scale on the standard MMPI-2 and MMPI-A profiles measuring gender-role reversal or nontraditional sex-role attitudes.

Mode. A statistical term indicating the most frequently occurring score or measurement in a distribution.

Neurotic triad. The three MMPI-2 and MMPI-A clinical scales Hs, D, and Hy.

Norm-referenced tests. Measures that compare test-takers with each other. Grading on a "curve" is an example of norm-referencing.

OBS or Obsessiveness scale. An MMPI-2 content scale.

O-H or Overcontrolled Hostility scale. This scale purports to assess overcontrol of hostile, aggressive behavior. It does not predict such behavior but explains it after it has occurred.

Pa or Paranoia scale (scale 6). An MMPI-2 and MMPI-A clinical scale measuring suspiciousness and paranoid ideation.

Pathognomonic symptom or sign. A sufficient indicant for assigning a particular diagnosis or classification (e.g., the use of MMPI-2 items as indicators of pathology such as suicidal thinking).

Pd or Psychopathic Deviate scale (scale 4). An MMPI-2 and MMPI-A clinical scale measuring antisocial behavior.

Percentile rank. The proportion of a group that falls below a particular point.

Percentile score. The rank from the bottom of a scale expressed as a percentage.

Percentile value of elevations. The percentage of cases that obtain scores at the T-score level obtained by the test-taker. The percentile values for various T-score levels are slightly different for men and women.

Men

T = 60	84.4 percentile
T = 65	92.4 percentile
T = 70	96.2 percentile
T = 75	98.2 percentile
T = 80	99.2 percentile
T = 85	99.7 percentile

Women

T = 60	84.9 percentile
T = 65	91.7 percentile
T = 70	95.8 percentile
T = 75	98.0 percentile
T = 80	99.3 percentile
T = 85	99.8 percentile

Personality disorder. A group of maladaptive behavioral syndromes originating in the developmental years (usually considered learning-based disorders), not characterized by neurotic or psychotic symptoms.

Prevalence. A statistical term referring to the total number of cases of a particular event or phenomenon within a specified time (see also **Incidence**).

Profile. A method of displaying test scores that provides a visual comparison of relative performance on scales.

Profile code. Also referred to as code type, an MMPI-2 based summary of scores that defines the most elevated scores in the profile, either a single scale score or a combination of several scale scores.

Profile configuration. The shape or pattern of MMPI-2 clinical scale scores on a given profile. For example, the 1-3 configuration is made up of elevations on Scales 1 (Hs) and 3 (Hy).

Profile definition. A term referring to how elevated the most elevated clinical scales are above the next highest scales in the profile. For example, if the two highest scales are ten or more T-score points above the third-ranked scale in the profile, the profile code is said to be *well defined* or to have *very high profile definition*; if a profile code is 5 to 9 T-score points higher than the next score, it is said to have *high profile definition*. Those profiles with 4 or fewer T-score points separating the code from the next score have *low profile definition*. Profiles with high or very high profile definition tend to be stable over time.

Profile elevation. The distance of a given MMPI-2 or MMPI-A T score from the mean score of "normals" expressed in T-score points. For example, a T score of 70 is elevated two full standard deviations above the mean score of the normative sample.

PSY-5 scales. A set of experimental MMPI-2 scales developed to assess the "five-factor" model of personality.

Psychophysiological (psychosomatic) disorders. Physical disorders in which psychological factors are considered to play a major causative role.

Pt or Psychasthenia scale (scale 7). An MMPI-2 and MMPI-A clinical scale measuring anxiety.

Random sample. A subgroup of a larger group (termed the population) selected in such a way that each member of the larger group has an equal probability of being chosen.

R or Repression scale (Welsh). A factor analytic scale on the MMPI-2 and MMPI-A that defines the second major factor of the item pools: overcontrol.

Rational scale development. A method of scale construction in which items are selected based on their face validity. This strategy involves "rational" or obvious content item selection procedures.

Reliability. The degree to which a test or other form of measurement is consistent in producing the same result every time it is used to assess or measure a particular person who has not changed significantly between testings (see Chapter 8).

Response rate. A statistical term for the percentage of those invited to participate in a study who actually participate. For example, if surveys were mailed to 200 randomly selected individuals and 150 individuals completed and returned the survey form, the response rate would be 75 percent.

Sc or Schizophrenia scale (scale 8). An MMPI-2 and MMPI-A clinical scale measuring bizarre thinking.

Scale. A systematic framework for assigning names or measurements.

Self-report questionnaire. A questionnaire or inventory designed to obtain self-descriptions from an individual.

Sensitivity. When a psychological test has been validated to identify a certain condition, sensitivity refers to the proportion of tested individuals who test positive, who actually have the condition (see **False negative, False positive,** and **Specificity**).

Si or Social Introversion scale (scale 0). An MMPI-2 and MMPI-A clinical scale measuring introversion.

Skewness. A statistical term indicating the degree to which measurements fall in a symmetrical (i.e., not skewed) or asymmetrical (i.e., skewed) pattern around the mean.

Social approval or social desirability bias. The tendency for an individual to provide answers that would be perceived as socially approved or socially desirable.

SOD or Social Discomfort scale. An MMPI-2 content scale.

Somatic. Relating to the body; for example, headaches and abdominal pain would be characterized as somatic complaints.

Specificity. If a psychological test has been validated to identify a certain condition, specificity refers to the proportion of tested individuals who test negative, who do not have the condition (see **False negative, False positive,** and **Sensitivity**).

Standard deviation. A statistical measure of the spread or dispersion of scores (or other measures) around the mean; the square root of the variance.

Standard score. A score (e.g., on a standardized psychological test) calculated in terms of standard deviations from the statistical mean of scores.

Submerged profile. A term describing a profile that has no points at or above a T score of 50.

Syndrome. A group or pattern of symptoms, sequelae, or characteristics of a disorder.

T scores. Scores falling along a distribution in which the mean is 50 and the standard deviation is 10.

Teleprocessing. A computer-based data processing procedure by which psychological tests are scored and interpreted through telephone link-up with a central processing center.

Test. A standardized procedure for obtaining observations or behaviors and describing them on a numerical scale or in categories.

Test user qualifications. Guidelines established by a professional organization (e.g., the American Psychological Association) specifying the level of training and experience required for a given test.

TPA or Type-A Personality scale. An MMPI-2 content scale.

TR (or T-R). Abbreviation for test-retest, a form of test reliability usually expressed as a correlation; changes in test scores for an individual test-taker may reflect the imperfect reliability of the test (generally chance or error variance), an actual change in the individual's condition, or the possibility that the individual is intentionally or unconsciously distorting responses but not in a consistent manner.

TRIN or True Response Inconsistency scale. An MMPI-2 and MMPI-A validity scale measuring inconsistency in terms of True responding (yea-saying) and False responding (nay-saying).

TRT or Negative Treatment Indicators scale. An MMPI-2 content scale.

Type I error. A research term indicating that a decision (in interpreting results) was made that there was an actual (i.e., not due to chance) difference or finding when in reality there was no such actual difference or finding; also known as alpha error.

Type II error. A research term indicating that a decision (in interpreting results) was made that there was no actual (i.e., not due to chance) difference or finding when in reality there was such a difference or finding; also known as beta error.

Uniform T scores. A statistical term (see **T scores**) for the type of scaling used in the MMPI-2 and MMPI-A resulting in comparable percentile values for a given T score across the clinical and content scales.

Validity. The degree to which a test or other form of measurement actually assesses or measures what it is designed to assess or measure.

Variable. A characteristic, attribute, or measurement that has at least two levels or categories. For example, "Work" can be divided into "paid" and "unpaid" (i.e., two levels), but it is also possible to define work as a variable with many more levels or categories ("hard," "medium," or "light," as experienced or defined by the individual doing the work).

Variance. A statistical measure of the spread or dispersion of scores (or other measures) around the mean; the square of the standard deviation.

VRIN or Variable Response Inconsistency scale. An MMPI-2 and MMPI-A validity scale measuring inconsistent responding.

WRK or Work Interference scale. An MMPI-2 content scale.

Z scores. Standardized scores falling along a distribution in which the mean is 0 and the standard deviation is 1.

References

Ben-Porath, Y. S., & Davis, D. (1996). *Case studies for interpreting MMPI-A.* Minneapolis: University of Minnesota Press.

Butcher, J. N. (1999). *A beginner's guide to the MMPI-2.* Washington, D.C.: American Psychological Association.

Butcher, J. N., & Williams, C. L. (1992). *User's guide for the Minnesota Report: Adolescent Interpretive System.* Minneapolis: National Computer Systems.

Butcher, J. N., et al. (2000). *International case studies on the MMPI-A: an objective approach.* Minneapolis: University of Minnesota Press.

Pope, K., Butcher, J. N., & Seelen, J. (2000). *The MMPI/MMPI-2 and MMPI-A in court.* Washington, D.C.: American Psychological Association.

Keys to Exercises

Section 1. MMPI-2 and MMPI-A Concepts

Part A

1. code type
2. Content scales
3. Scale 1 Hypochondriasis (Hs)
4. Critical
5. content scales
6. base rate
7. empirical correlates
8. uniform T scores
9. addiction proneness
10. empirical scale construction
11. profile definition
12. configuration
13. definition
14. face
15. linear
16. code type
17. behavioral correlates
18. content scales; critical items
19. Actuarial prediction
20. linear T scores
21. criterion group
22. neurotic triad
23. 14; 18
24. 800
25. 2,600
26. Uniform
27. external correlates
28. +
29. *
30. three
31. percentile rank
32. are
33. 370
34. 350
35. Megargee Offender Classification System
36. average profile elevation

37. content
38. Actuarial prediction
39. uniform
40. 92d
41. Content scales
42. addiction proneness
43. external validity
44. supplementary scales
45. face validity
46. cut-off
47. two
48. submerged
49. checkmark validity pattern
50. floating

Part B

1. AAS
2. Hs; Hy
3. DEP; D (Depression)
4. anxiety
5. MDS
6. CYN
7. Hs
8. Pa
9. L
10. Ma (Hypomania)
11. Pa
12. Mf
13. Si
14. K
15. S (Superlative Self-Presentation)
16. VRIN
17. A-las
18. FAM
19. Sc
20. addiction proneness
21. masculine-feminine interests
22. Pd
23. .4K
24. .5K
25. 1K

26. are not
27. F; K
28. 80
29. Cannot Say scores
30. false
31. S, K
32. F_p
33. VRIN
34. F_p
35. acknowledgment of substance abuse problems
36. superlative self-presentation
37. infrequency
38. Ho
39. A
40. R
41. MDS
42. Pa
43. Pt
44. Si
45. low self-esteem
46. A-con
47. ACK
48. A-sch
49. addiction proneness
50. A-biz

Section 2. Plotting and Coding Profiles

Case 1

Part A. The values of K to be added to the scales are as follows. Refer to the box on the left of the hand-scoring profile sheet in Figure 1.

$$Hs = 13$$
$$Pd = 10$$
$$Pt = 25$$
$$Sc = 25$$
$$Ma = 5$$

Part B. The profile code is <u>643</u>+7-18<u>25</u>/09: LK'+-/:F# (D/0)

Part C. 6-4, two-point code type, but Scale 3 should also be considered in the interpretation.

Case 2

Part A. No K correction is included on MMPI-A profiles.

Part B. The profile code is 4"37'618+9-25/0 F/KL: (D/1)

Part C. 4-3, two-point code type; however, Scale 7 is also elevated and important to consider in the interpretation.

Section 3. Interpreting Profile Validity

Case 3

Scale		(a) Level	(b) Decision
?	Cannot Say	0	Clearly valid
VRIN	Variable Response Inconsistency	54	Clearly valid
TRIN	True Response Inconsistency	57F	Clearly valid
F	Infrequency	48	Clearly valid
F_b	Infrequency Back	42	Clearly valid
F_p	Infrequency Psychopathology	56	Clearly valid
L	Lie	70	Highly elevated, questionable validity
K	Defensiveness	68	Moderately elevated, possibly invalid
S	Superlative Self-Presentation	60	Somewhat elevated, interpretable

(c) In summary, this MMPI-2 validity pattern reveals a likely invalid protocol. The high L and K show excessive defensiveness and self-protection through the claiming of extreme virtues and the denial of any problems.

Case 4

Scale		(a) Level	(b) Decision
?	Cannot Say	0	Clearly valid
VRIN	Variable Response Inconsistency	50	Clearly valid
TRIN	True Response Inconsistency	73F	Moderately elevated, probably interpretable
F	Infrequency	79	Moderately elevated, probably interpretable
F_b	Infrequency Back	74	Moderately elevated, probably interpretable
F_p	Infrequency Psychopathology	49	Clearly valid
L	Lie	38	Clearly valid
K	Defensiveness	37	Clearly valid
S	Superlative Self-Presentation	35	Clearly valid

(c) In summary, this MMPI-2 pattern is an open presentation of symptoms. The client has endorsed a number of extreme symptoms but did not invalidate the protocol. There was also some tendency toward inconsistent responding in the false direction.

Case 5

Scale		(a) Level	(b) Decision
?	Cannot Say	0	Clearly valid
VRIN	Variable Response Inconsistency	47	Clearly valid
TRIN	True Response Inconsistency	53	Clearly valid
F	Infrequency	46	Clearly valid
F_1	Infrequency 1	42	Clearly valid
F_2	Infrequency 2	43	Clearly valid
L	Lie	59	Probably valid
K	Defensiveness	69	Moderately elevated, probably interpretable

(c) In summary, most of the MMPI-A validity indicators were clearly within the interpretable range. There was a moderate elevation on K, suggesting the need to consider this test performance as somewhat defensive. Any clinical scale elevations would be interpreted, however.

Case 6

Scale		(a) Level	(b) Decision
?	Cannot Say	0	Clearly valid
VRIN	Variable Response Inconsistency	40	Clearly valid
TRIN	True Response Inconsistency	53	Clearly valid
F_1	Infrequency 1	105	Highly elevated, probably invalid
F_2	Infrequency 2	70	Moderately elevated
F	Infrequency	86	Highly elevated, possibly invalid
L	Lie	43	Clearly valid
K	Defensiveness	40	Clearly valid

(c) In summary, this MMPI-A is likely to be invalid as a result of indiscriminate symptom endorsement.

Section 4. Interpreting the Clinical Scales

Case 7

Validity Scales

His performance on the MMPI-2 validity scales shows a somewhat defensive approach to the testing. This client attempted to present himself in a very favorable light, minimizing problems or psychological weakness.

Symptoms and Behavior from the Clinical Scales

Suggested Case Description for the Clinical Profile

The clinical scale prototype used in the development of this narrative includes a prominent elevation on

Scale Pd. The client is somewhat immature and impulsive, a risk-taker who may do things others do not approve of just for the personal enjoyment of doing so. He is likely to be viewed as rebellious. He tends to be generally oriented toward pleasure seeking and self-gratification. He may occasionally show bad judgment and tends to be somewhat self-centered, pleasure-oriented, narcissistic, and manipulative. He is not particularly anxious and shows no neurotic symptoms. Some individuals with this profile pattern engage in antisocial acts.

Individuals with this profile pattern may be seen by others initially as likable and personable and may make a good first impression. The client is typically outgoing, and his social behavior is not likely to change if he is retested at a later time. His personal relationships are likely to be somewhat superficial. He appears to be rather spontaneous and expressive and may seek attention from others, especially to gain social recognition.

His tendency to take personal risks and to act out at times may make it somewhat difficult for him to maintain close relationships. Persons with this pattern are often viewed as manipulative in social relationships.

Case 8

Validity Scales

The applicant approached the MMPI-2 in a generally frank and open manner. His MMPI-2 profile is probably a good indication of his present personality functioning.

Symptoms and Behavior from the Clinical Scales

Suggested Case Description for the Clinical Profile

The applicant's performance on the MMPI-2 suggests that he is outgoing and considers himself to have few psychological problems. His overuse of denial and his tendency to overextend himself may occasionally cause problems, however. He tends to be very aggressive, overconfident, and somewhat self-centered, with an unrealistic view of his capabilities. At times he is overly optimistic, fails to recognize his own limitations, and is insensitive to the needs of others. He tends to be an expressive spontaneous person who might act or make decisions without careful consideration of the consequences. Without apparent cause he may become somewhat elated, and at other times he may be moody and irritable.

He seems to lack the broad cultural interests characteristic of many individuals with this level of education. He appears to have a rather limited range of interests and prefers traditional, action-oriented activities to artistic and literary pursuits or introspective experiences. He may be somewhat intolerant and insensitive, and others may view him as rather crude, coarse, and narrow-minded.

He appears to be a very outgoing person, forward and aggressive in relationships and able to influence others easily. Although he makes a good first impression and probably makes friends easily, his relationships tend to be rather superficial. Quite outgoing and sociable, he has a strong need to be around other people. He appears to be quite gregarious and seems to need social recognition. Such individuals tend to be spontaneous and socially expressive. At times he may engage in behavior to attract attention.

Case 9

Validity Scales

The adolescent's performance on the MMPI-A validity scales was open and cooperative. His MMPI-A clinical profile is likely to be a good indication of his present personality functioning.

Symptoms and Behavior from the Clinical Scales

This adolescent's MMPI-A clinical profile reflects a high degree of psychological distress at this time. He appears rather tense and depressed and may be feeling agitated over problems in his environment. He may be experiencing a great deal of stress following a period of acting-out behavior, possibly including problem use of alcohol or other drugs. He appears to be developing a pattern of poor impulse control and a lack of acceptance of societal standards. This individual may also be angry about his present situation and may blame others for his problems. He may be seeking a temporary respite from situational stress. He may attempt to manipulate others through his symptoms to escape responsibility for the problems he has created.

He endorsed an unusual pattern of interests compared to other young men his age. He acknowledged interests that seem more stereotypically feminine and denied interests that are traditionally masculine.

Symptoms of depression are quite prominent in his responses to the MMPI-A. He reports sadness, fatigue, crying spells, and self-deprecatory thoughts. His life may seem uninteresting and not worthwhile. Feelings of loneliness, pessimism, and uselessness are prominent.

His relationships may be somewhat superficial. He may use others for his own gratification. He is somewhat hedonistic and may act out impulsively without due concern for the feelings of friends or relatives. He has probably been experiencing strained interpersonal relationships.

He is somewhat shy, with some social anxiety and inhibitions. He is a bit hypersensitive about what others think of him and is occasionally concerned about his relationships with others. He appears to be somewhat inhibited in personal relationships and social situations, and he may have some difficulty expressing his feelings toward others. He may try to avoid crowds, parties, or school activities.

Case 10

Validity Scales

The adolescent's approach to the MMPI-A was open and cooperative. The resulting MMPI-A is valid and is probably a good indication of her present level of personality functioning. This may be viewed as a positive indication of her involvement with the evaluation.

Symptoms and Behavior from the Clinical Scales

This adolescent's MMPI-A clinical profile indicates multiple serious behavior problems, including school maladjustment, family discord, and authority conflicts. She can be moody, resentful, and attention seeking. At times she may appear rebellious, impulsive, and argumentative. Her poor judgment may get her into trouble. She can be self-centered and may show little remorse for her bad behavior. She may run away or lie to avoid punishment. Individuals with this MMPI-A pattern tend to be impulsive, show poor judgment, and get into difficulties with authorities.

She may initially seem likable and may make a good impression on others; however, her relationships tend to be very troubled. Her behavior is primarily hedonistic and self-centered, and she is quite insensitive to the needs of others, exploiting them and feeling no guilt over it.

Section 5. Interpreting the Content Scales

Case 11

The content themes that the client reported are summarized as follows.

She has reported that she feels very uneasy around others and prefers to be by herself much of the time. In social situations she is likely to sit by herself rather than join the group. She views herself as shy and as disliking social events.

She has reported that she is experiencing symptoms of anxiety, tension, and somatic problems. She has reported sleeping problems, worries, and poor concentration. She has acknowledged that she fears losing her mind sometimes and usually feels that life is a strain. She has difficulty making decisions. She appears to be readily aware of these symptoms and is open to admitting them.

She has acknowledged considerable family discord. She is described as lacking in love, quarrelsome, and unpleasant. She acknowledges that she hates members of her family. She feels that her family is lacking in affection.

She acknowledges having many physical symptoms that cross several body systems, including gastrointestinal symptoms (e.g., constipation, nausea and vomiting, stomach trouble), neurological problems (e.g., convulsions, dizzy and fainting spells, paralysis), sensory problems (e.g., poor hearing and eyesight), cardiovascular symptoms (e.g., heart or chest pains), skin problems, pain (e.g., headaches, neck pains), respiratory troubles (e.g., coughs, hay fever or asthma). She worries a great deal about her health and feels that her health is not as good as most other people's.

She also reports feeling depressed. She feels uncertain about her future and is uninterested in much that is going on around her. She broods a lot and feels unhappy, hopeless, and empty. She is likely to cry a great deal and may have thoughts of suicide or wish that she were dead. She views other people as unsupportive.

Case 12

The content themes that the client reported are summarized as follows.

In addition to any interpretations on the MMPI-2 validity and clinical scale scores, Charlie has expressed a number of problems through the MMPI-2 item content. He feels that his home life is unpleasant and he does not expect it to improve. Any psychological intervention will need to focus on his negative family feelings if treatment is to progress. He has difficulty managing routine affairs, and the items he endorsed suggest that he is reporting signs of poor memory, concentration problems, and an inability to make decisions. He appears to be immobilized and withdrawn and has no energy for life. He views his physical health as failing and reports numerous somatic concerns. He feels that life is no longer worthwhile and that he is losing control of his thought processes. He views the world as a threatening place, sees himself as having been unjustly blamed for others' problems, and feels that he is getting a raw deal out of life.

Case 13

The content themes that the client reported can be summarized as follows.

She reports that she feels very depressed at this time. She acknowledges that she is experiencing symptoms of low mood, sadness, tension, and somatic problems. She reports fatigue, crying spells, and self-deprecatory thoughts. She has reported sleeping problems, worries, and poor concentration. She has acknowledged that she has difficulty making decisions. She appears to be readily aware of these symptoms and is open to admitting them.

She has acknowledged that she is experiencing considerable discord with her parents and other family members. She described her family as lacking in love, quarrelsome, and unpleasant. She acknowledges that she hates some members of her family and feels that her family is lacking in affection. She has endorsed some item content suggesting conduct problems. The possibility that she is or has engaged in aggressive, antisocial acts should be followed up. She has reported a number of problems related to having difficulties in school. She probably has poor academic performance and does not participate in school activities. She may have a history of truancy or suspensions from school. She likely has very negative attitudes about school and reports that the only positive aspect of school is being with her friends.

She endorsed some items that indicate possible difficulty in establishing a therapeutic relationship. She may be reluctant to self-disclose in therapy, she may be distrustful of helping professionals, and she may believe that her problems cannot be solved.

Case 14

The content themes that the client reported can be summarized as follows.

His MMPI-A content scales profile reveals important areas to consider in his evaluation. He reports many behavioral problems, including stealing, shoplifting, lying, breaking or destroying property, being disrespectful, swearing, or being oppositional. He may belong to a peer group that is frequently in trouble and encourages deviant behavior. Poor academic performance and behavioral problems in school are also possible.

He reports numerous difficulties in school. He probably has poor academic performance and does not participate in school activities. He may have a history of truancy or suspensions from school. He probably has very negative attitudes about school, possibly reporting that the only positive aspect of school is being with his friends. He reports very limited interest in school or investment in success. He does not expect to succeed in life. He reports disliking reading and studying, and he may be seen as "lazy." He has difficulty starting projects, tends to give up easily, and allows others to take charge.

Section 6. Interpreting Supplementary or Special Scales

Case 15

The supplementary scale elevations can be summarized as follows.

The client is experiencing a high degree of stress at this time as noted by her extremely elevated score on the PTSD scale. She worries a great deal, is tense, and is unhappy with her current life situation. Some individuals with her MMPI-2 performance have recently experienced extremely stressful or traumatic situations.

In addition, she has a number of personality characteristics that are associated with the development of addictive disorders (APS at a T score of 60). Moreover, she acknowledged some problems with alcohol or drug abuse on the AAS scale. A substance abuse evaluation should explore the extent to which her functioning is impaired as a result of alcohol or drug use.

Case 16

The supplementary scale elevations can be summarized as follows.

The client shows a pattern of likely addiction proneness in the context of substance use/abuse denial. His high score on the APS scale indicates that he has endorsed many items that persons in substance abuse treatment programs endorse. He does not appear to be willing to acknowledge use or abuse of alcohol or drugs, however, as noted by the relatively low score on AAS.

Case 17

The MMPI-A supplementary scale elevations can be summarized as follows.

Two of the three substance abuse indicators suggest that the patient is likely to be having serious alcohol or drug abuse problems. The PRO scale suggests that she is likely to be involved with a peer group that uses alcohol and drugs. She has acknowledged alcohol and drug use, although she tends to be a person who uses repression and overcontrol of emotions.

Case 18

The MMPI-A supplementary scale elevations can be summarized as follows. See Ben-Porath & Davis (1996) for a more complete evaluation of this case.

Although many aspects of this profile appear to be a "call for help" in that the client is presenting a large number of symptoms, the supplementary scales suggest a somewhat less than forthcoming problem admission. On both the MAC-R and the PRO scale she appears to have a very high potential for developing a substance abuse disorder; however, she appears not to admit use or resulting problems frankly, as noted by the relatively low score on ACK. In any treatment intervention, the psychologist should confront the disparity in these scale scores and discuss further with her the indications of a developing addictive disorder. Her performance on the Repression scale suggests that she may tend to deal with conflict by overcontrol and repression. The possibility that she does not face up to her problems directly should be further evaluated.

Section 7. Profile Interpretation

Case 19

The client's MMPI-2 performance can be summarized as follows.

Profile Validity

The MMPI-2 profile is valid. The client was sufficiently cooperative with the evaluation to produce an interpretable profile. There was some tendency on her part to be overly frank and to exaggerate her present symptoms, but this does not invalidate the test results.

Symptomatic Pattern

The client's MMPI-2 suggests the presence of a number of personality and symptom problems. Her personality problems include impulsive behavior, poor judgment, aggression, and acting-out behavior. She shows a chronic pattern of behavior that is highly resistant to change. Persons with this clinical profile tend to behave irresponsibly at times and blame others for their problems. There is a strong hedonistic quality to her behavior; she is likely to seek pleasure at any cost. There is a strong possibility that she overuses alcohol or drugs.

In addition to the personality problems indicated, she is depressed at this time. Her mood symptoms may be related to stressful factors in her present environment. In her response to items she also presented herself as having anger control problems. At times she appears to have a high potential for explosive behavior. She endorsed statements that indicate some inability to control her anger. She may physically or verbally attack others when she is angry.

Interpersonal Relationships

Individuals with this MMPI-2 pattern tend to manipulate others in interpersonal contexts. Her hedonistic lifestyle probably centers on manipulating other people to get her way. She obtained a very high score on the Marital Distress Scale, indicating that she has many problems in her marriage. She also reports extensive family relationship difficulties. She feels intensely angry, hostile, and resentful toward others, and she would like to get back at other people. She is competitive and uncooperative and tends to be very critical of others.

Diagnostic Considerations

Several factors need to be considered when developing a diagnostic formulation. She shows strong antisocial behavioral features and likely substance abuse. She also reports substantial difficulty in interpersonal relationships and anger toward others. In addition, she shows some indication of having a comorbid affective disorder at this time. She reports significant depression, perhaps in relation to lifestyle problems.

Treatment Considerations

Individuals with this MMPI-2 pattern typically do not respond well to psychological treatment. They are usually not insight oriented and tend to have numerous relationship problems that are resistant to treatment. Persons with this profile tend to act out their problems and conflicts in antisocial ways rather than resolve them.

Case 20

The adolescent tested in this case is from Peru and was administered the MMPI-A in Spanish. The MMPI-A was interpreted using the computer-based Minnesota Report for adolescents based on American norms.

The Minnesota Report

Validity Considerations

This is a valid MMPI-A. She is neither denying problems nor claiming an excessive number of unusual symptoms. Her low K score suggests an overly frank self-appraisal, possibly presenting a more negative picture than is warranted. This may reflect a need to get attention for her problems.

Symptomatic Behavior

Adolescents with this clinical scales profile show an extreme pattern of psychological maladjustment that combines acting-out problems with more neurotic and dependent behaviors. This individual tends to be quite oppositional, resistant, sneaky, and underhanded. She can be overemotional when things don't go her way. Her behavior is unpredictable and she is very moody. She may tease, bully, or dominate her peers. Anger-control problems may be pronounced. She may have problems with alcohol or other drugs, and she may have difficulties in school. More serious antisocial problems, including acting out sexually, are possible.

She can also be very clinging and dependent on adults (e.g., seeking their help, wanting to be around them). She may be troubled by beliefs that she is evil or deserves severe punishment. These ideas may take on an obsessional quality. Paradoxically, she also tends to externalize blame.

The highest clinical scale in her MMPI-A clinical profile, Pd, occurs with very high frequency in adolescent alcohol/drug or psychiatric treatment units. Over 24 percent of girls in treatment settings have this well-defined peak score (i.e., with the Pd scale at least 5 points higher than the next scale). The Pd scale is among the least frequently occurring peak elevations in the normative girls' sample (about 3 percent).

Her MMPI-A content scales profile reveals important areas to consider in her evaluation. She reports several strange thoughts and experiences, which may include hallucinations, persecutory ideas, or feelings of being controlled by others. She may worry that something is wrong with her mind.

She reports many behavioral problems, including stealing, shoplifting, lying, breaking or destroying property, being disrespectful, swearing, or being oppositional. She may belong to a peer group that is frequently in trouble and encourages deviant behavior. Poor academic performance and behavioral problems in school are also possible, as are behavior problems at home. She may be sexually active, flirtatious, provocative, or promiscuous.

Symptoms of depression are quite prominent in her responses to the MMPI-A. She reports sadness, fatigue, crying spells, and self-deprecatory thoughts. Her life may seem uninteresting and not worthwhile. Feelings of loneliness, pessimism, and uselessness are prominent.

She reported numerous problems in school, both academic and behavioral. She reported several symptoms of anxiety, including tension, worries, and difficulties sleeping.

Interpersonal Relations

She has a great deal of difficulty in her social relationships. She feels that others do not understand her and do not give her enough sympathy. She is somewhat aloof, cold, nongiving, and uncompromising, attempting to advance herself at the expense of others. She tends to be hostile, resentful, and irritable.

Some interpersonal issues are suggested by her MMPI-A content scales profile. Family problems are quite significant in her life. She reports numerous problems with her parents and other family members. She describes her family in terms of discord, jealousy, fault finding, anger, serious disagreements, lack of love and understanding, and very limited communication. She looks forward to the day when she can leave home for good, and she does not feel that she can count on her family in times of trouble. Her parents and she often disagree about her friends. She indicates that her parents treat her like a child and frequently punish her without cause. Her family problems probably have a negative effect on her behavior in school. This young person reports feeling distant from others. Other people seem unsympathetic toward her. She feels unliked and believes that no one understands her. She reported some irritability and impatience with others. She may have problems controlling her anger.

Behavioral Stability

The relative scale elevation of the highest scales (Pd, Pa) in her clinical profile reflects high profile definition. If she is retested at a later date, the peak scores on this test are likely to retain their relative salience in her profile pattern. This adolescent's acting-out behaviors and extreme dependency needs may produce periods of intense interpersonal difficulty.

Diagnostic Considerations

An individual with this MMPI-A clinical scales profile may be viewed as developing characteristics of a personality problem. Externalizing behaviors are likely to be prominent in her clinical pattern. She admits to having some symptoms of eating disorders (e.g., binging, purging, or laxative use for weight loss). She reported several bizarre thoughts and behaviors. If these experiences cannot be explained by alcohol or other drug intoxication, organic problems, a misunderstanding of the items, or an intentional exaggeration of psychopathology, a psychotic process should be considered. Her highly elevated Conduct Problems scale may indicate the presence of an oppositional-defiant disorder or a conduct disorder. Given her elevation on the School Problems scale, her diagnostic evaluation could include assessment of possible academic skills deficits and behavior problems.

She obtained extremely high scores on all three of the alcohol- and drug-problem scales, indicative of serious problems in this area. She probably engages in risk-taking behaviors and tends toward exhibitionism. She probably belongs to a peer group who uses alcohol or other drugs. Her involvement in an alcohol- or drug-using lifestyle should be further evaluated. She has acknowledged having alcohol- or drug-abuse problems in her responses to the MMPI-A. Problems at home or school are likely, given her problems with alcohol or other drugs.

Treatment Considerations

The MMPI-A clinical scales profile suggests that this individual has serious problems that require intervention. She will probably be a difficult therapy patient because of her distrust, moodiness, and potential for acting out. A supportive, consistent approach may be helpful. A directive strategy focusing on behavioral change may prove more beneficial than insight-oriented techniques. Her dependency needs may be an asset in building a therapeutic relationship; however, the relationship may be stormy at times, with the therapist being inundated with unrealistic demands.

Her very high potential for developing alcohol or drug problems requires attention in therapy if important life changes are to be made. She has acknowledged some problems in this area, which is a valuable first step for intervention.

She should be evaluated for the presence of suicidal thoughts and any possible suicidal behaviors. If she is at risk, appropriate precautions should be taken.

Her family situation, which is full of conflict, should be considered in her treatment planning. Family therapy may be helpful if her parents or guardians are willing and able to work on conflict resolution. If family therapy is not feasible, it may be profitable during the course of her treatment to explore her substantial anger at and disappointment in her family. Alternate sources of emotional support from adults (e.g., foster parent, teacher, other relative, friend's parent, or neighbor) could be explored and facilitated in the absence of caring parents.

There are some symptom areas suggested by the content scales profile that the therapist may wish to consider in initial treatment sessions. Her endorsement of internalizing symptoms of anxiety and depression could be explored further.

During the course of her treatment, it may be important to discuss her sexual behavior. Her knowledge about sexuality and protecting herself against sexually transmitted diseases could be assessed and information provided, if needed. Perhaps in a trusting therapeutic relationship she will be able to discuss the extent of her sexual activity and its meaning in her life. Alternatives to risky, promiscuous behavior could be discussed and promoted. If she is flirtatious and provocative, a greater awareness of this on her part may prevent unwanted sexual advances or possible victimization. Social skills training may be helpful in changing possibly inappropriate behaviors.

She may have several attitudes and beliefs that could interfere with establishing a therapeutic relationship. These may include very negative opinions about mental health professionals, an unwillingness to self-disclose, and beliefs that her problems are unsolvable. She may be unwilling to accept responsibility for her behaviors or to plan for her future. She may doubt that others care enough to help her or that they are capable of understanding her.

This adolescent's emotional distance and discomfort in interpersonal situations must be considered in developing a treatment plan. She may have difficulty self-disclosing, especially in groups. She may not appreciate receiving feedback from others about her behavior or problems.

James N. Butcher is professor of psychology at the University of Minnesota. He is author of numerous articles and books on the MMPI instruments. He served on the MMPI-2 Restandardization Committee and is the MMPI consultant to the University of Minnesota Press. He has conducted the workshop series Symposia of Recent Development in the Use of the MMPI for thirty-five years.